"Ruth Haley Barton's book is timely and essential reading for all women who struggle to any degree with the restrictions they find imposed upon them by their own thinking and that of the world around them, including that of the church. Through the narration of her own struggle and search to find freedom as a Christian woman, Ruth brings new insight into well-worn biblical passages in a way that will transform your thinking forever. Christ came to set us free, and if you want to be free indeed, then Ruth's inspired, challenging, yet devotional book is all you've been waiting for. I can't recommend it more highly—give one to every woman you know, and then watch God change the world!"

ALIE STIBBE AUTHOR OF *BAREFOOT IN THE KITCHEN* (BRF 2004)

"I finished reading *Longing for More* in the first days of caring for my newborn daughter—a perfect time to think, dream and pray about her life as a beloved daughter of God. Ruth Haley Barton's book was a thought-provoking companion for this journey. I hope many women—and men—will read it slowly and prayerfully."

AMY BOUCHER PYE, EDITOR AND COLUMNIST, *WOMAN ALIVE* AND *CHRISTIAN MARKETPLACE*

"Ruth deals with many issues that are familiar to women in the Western evangelical church. But her approach is fresh and honest. Many of us have grown weary in the battle to use the gifts God has given us. So I found Ruth's encouragement to be truthful and to break out of the traditional moulds—either ideological or theological—very helpful. She warns us that this could be risky and a tough route, as she herself found. But she also helps us see that to be true to our gifting and calling we need a major re-think and re-orientation—and prepare for the tears. But it is all in context of the huge calling we have in Christ. I am so grateful for the realism and scope of this book, and the thorough biblical framework for all she says."

SHEENA GILLIES, A MEMBER OF THE MINISTRY STAFF AT ST JAMES CHURCH, CLERKENWELL

"I see dozens of women who are walking a straight line to frustration and bitterness. *Longing for More* really could bring them freedom. Ruth Haley Barton offers a straight line—a narrow but liberating way—to joy in the Spirit."

DR. LARRY CRABB, AUTHOR OF *SHATTERED DREAMS* AND *THE PRESSURE'S OFF*

"With an honest voice, Ruth Barton helps women move away from small ideas of what we should be, think and do, and instead embrace the enormity of our calling in Christ. This book is an invitation to drink in the rich truths that free us to live as his disciples in the whole of our life—in marriage, motherhood, friendships, and in service to the church and the world."

ANDI ASHWORTH, AUTHOR OF *REAL LOVE FOR REAL LIFE: THE ART AND WORK OF CARING*

"This book is a substantive, gut-level, practical and well-researched piece of writing that deals with real-life issues from a vibrantly biblical perspective. To women and men who are confused by the welter of conflicting definitions of gender, roles and sexuality that is currently thrown at them, the author offers excellent, biblically grounded guidance for the development of authentic Christian womanhood. I predict that this work will become a classic textbook for Christians in quest of wholesome, God-honoring, biblically accurate answers to some of the most urgent personal issues of the day."

DR. GILBERT BILEZIKIAN, PROFESSOR EMERITUS OF BIBLICAL STUDIES, WHEATON COLLEGE, AND AUTHOR OF *BEYOND SEX ROLES*

"This is a book filled with wisdom, truth-telling, encouragement and practical help for today's Christian woman struggling with issues of marriage and parenting, identity and work, as she seeks to know and follow Jesus. I found it enjoyable reading as well as challenging."

REV. DR. ROBERTA HESTENES, MINISTER-AT-LARGE WITH WORLD VISION INTERNATIONAL AND FOUNDER OF THE HESTENES CENTER FOR CHRISTIAN WOMEN IN LEADERSHIP

"I have often wished that women would tell each other the truth—that we would not stand idly by and watch our sisters scrounge around in the dirt of trial and error searching for answers. I am deeply grateful to Ruth Haley Barton for being brave, honest and loving enough to share *Longing for More* with all who seek to know a God who gives us the courage to be our best selves."

REV. BRENDA SALTER MCNEIL, AUTHOR OF *THE HEART OF RACIAL JUSTICE*

Longing for More

Ruth Haley Barton

*A woman's
path to transformation
in Christ*

INTER-VARSITY PRESS
Norton Street, Nottingham NG7 3HR, England
Email: ivp@ivpbooks.com
Website: www.ivpbooks.com

First published 2007

British Library Cataloguing in Publication Data
A catalogue record for this book is available from the British Library.

ISBN 978-1-84474-205-9

Typeset in the USA
Printed in Great Britain by Ashford Colour Press Ltd, Gosport, Hampshire

Inter-Varsity Press publishes Christian books that are true to the Bible and that communicate the gospel, develop
discipleship and strengthen the church for its mission in the world.

Inter-Varsity Press is closely linked with the Universities and Colleges Christian Fellowship, a student movement
connecting Christian Unions in universities and colleges throughout Great Britain, and a member movement of the
International Fellowship of Evangelical Students. Website: www.uccf.org.uk

To my daughters:

Charity Ruth, Bethany Joy and Haley Hope

It is one of the greatest privileges of my life

to share the journey of spiritual transformation with you.

Contents

Foreword

I am reading the manuscript of *Longing for More* on a train en route from Dublin to Belfast. I have just visited with a dear Irish friend, a woman preparing—as I am—to enter the decade of her fifties. Last evening, as we sat under a full moon in the garden of a quaint hotel in County Wicklow, we compared notes on the busy, domestic years of our twenties and thirties when our lives revolved around the needs of our children and our husbands. Then we talked about the transitional challenges of our forties, when suddenly it seemed we received the long-desired gift of discretionary time but then had no clue what to do with it. Finally, we shared with each other our dreams of the future, shadowy at this point but offering us just enough definition to allow us to begin taking active, preparatory steps.

This morning, as I sit here reading Ruth's manuscript, I can't help but think how much my Irish friend and I would have benefited from this book twenty-five years ago when we were young women making choices about our future. And as the train rumbles along, I find myself wishing that I had about two hundred copies of the completed book stashed away in my suitcase. I would love to be able to stack them on the booktable at the conference in Belfast where I am scheduled to speak in the coming days. In fact, I would probably be tempted to say, "Hey, don't bother to sit through my talk. Just buy Ruth's book."

I should not be surprised that this book compellingly reinforces—and pushes to greater depth—the same themes that I seek to embrace more fully in my own life and to communicate to other women. The ongoing friendship and dialogue that Ruth and I have enjoyed in recent years has shown us to be kindred spirits in many ways. We are of one mind, from our shared belief that silence can lead us into the heart of God to our shared conviction that women—strong in the strength God has given us—have the potential to change the world.

The spiritual exercises at the end of each chapter confirm truths that I have found strength in over the years. I have learned that there is great power in personal prayer and reflective journaling. I've also experienced the equal power of prayerful listening and discussion in a small community of women who are earnestly seeking the guidance of God. I'm glad that Ruth leads us into both.

As I was reading this manuscript I circled many paragraphs, scribbled down many quotes and scattered hundreds of exclamation points in the margins—but I keep going back to one line in particular: "It is time," writes Ruth, "to stand for what you believe and never look back." I spent many years of my adult life plagued by fear and by a litany of falsehoods. In the future I want to stand strongly and firmly on the side of courage, on the side of truth, on the side of goodness, on the side of the revolutionary gospel of Jesus. *Longing for More* challenges, encourages, motivates and empowers me toward that end. Thank you, Ruth.

Lynne Hybels

An Invitation to Transformation in Christ

The freedom question, then, is not whether we can do whatever we want but whether we can do what we most deeply want.

GERALD MAY, *THE AWAKENED HEART*

It used to be that a woman's choices were fairly simple: she went to school, got married, stayed married to the same man—for better or worse—and raised children. There were standards of conduct and morality that were widely accepted, and generally we knew what was expected.

This is no longer the case. Today we can have a career, full time or part time, at home or away from home, or we can focus our energy and time solely on family and volunteer work. We can get married or stay single. We can have children—or not. The choice to have children leads to further choices: about whether to adopt or whether to choose any of a myriad of reproductive options available today. But choices do not necessarily make life easier—they often make life *more difficult,* because they produce guilt, self-doubt and stress. With increased options comes an increased awareness of the possibility for making mistakes, and this awareness can produce real anxiety.

On the other hand, more choices also yield increased opportunities for *good* options—options for spending our time, energy and resources in ways that are life-giving for us and our world. These new
possibilities touch our longing to make a difference and to know that
our presence on this planet matters. These "choice points" include
but go far beyond issues such as dating, career, marriage, children
and money. Underlying these obvious concerns are the more subtle
choices regarding our values, moral and ethical standards, life calling, and belief system. We look for role models who have successfully
negotiated the twists, turns and pitfalls of the road, yet we're not sure
whose wisdom and insight to trust.

Celebrities on their second or third marriage are anxious to tell us
how to have a happy marriage. We listen in as sports figures and successful businesspeople share their secrets of success, only to find out
later that their personal lives are fraught with immorality or addic-
tions. Psychologists and other experts give advice on every issue from
morality to childrearing. Add to these the plethora of friends, family
and religious influences—all offering ideas about who women ought
to be and what they ought to do—and things can become so confusing that it is tempting to give up and take the path of least resistance.

Of course, some of these sources do have valuable advice to offer,
but even the best advice does not necessarily represent that which is
most deeply called for in our own life. We are almost persuaded—
but not quite. To make matters more complicated, young women today have had the chance to observe the previous generation's choices
and are finding the results to be decidedly mixed. When we are honest, many of us admit to feelings of ambivalence about the choices
women have made over the years.

In the 1960s women witnessed the power of choice as our sisters
burned their bras and fought for equal rights. In the 1970s and early

1980s women experienced the initial euphoria of having the opportunity to get out there and prove what we could do. But as the late 1980s wore on into the 1990s, the euphoria wore off, and we began to experience a new realism about choices we had made. Reluctantly we began to admit to a new set of questions and concerns. Now in this new millennium we recognize some of the discoveries we've made.

1. *Most have learned the hard way that there's no such thing as Superwoman.* The physical exhaustion that many of us have experienced from managing a home and career has helped us to see our limitations.

2. *Many have experienced guilt and sadness as a result of our choices.* Our small children hold on tight and cry when we have to leave for work. We find it very hard to keep up with friendships. On the other hand, those of us who are stay-at-home moms wonder if we are failing to develop our gifts and fulfill our potential.

3. *Our choices have brought a sense of disillusionment.* In her article "The Failure of Feminism," Kay Ebeling observes, "In general, feminism gave men all the financial and personal advantages over women. What's worse, we asked for it. The reality of feminism is a lot of frenzied and overworked women dropping kids off at daycare centers."

4. *We've realized that choosing one thing means saying no to something else.* An executive vice president of a Fortune 500 company acknowledges the price she has paid to get where she has gotten. "I don't take care of the house. I don't cook. I don't market. I don't take my children to the malls and museums. And I don't have close friends. I am frequently too tired to tell my husband about my day . . . or to play with the children."

5. *There is an uncertainty that underlies our confidence.* Peggy Orenstein describes our situation at the beginning of a new century as "a

state of flux." She points out that "Old patterns and expectations
have broken down, but new ideas seem fragmentary, unrealistic,
and often contradictory."

Even as we talk about all the options women have today, many
times we feel that our own choices are limited. In fact, at times in all
of our lives we feel downright stuck. We don't have all the choices we
would like to have—choices about income level, how we are treated
by our husband, educational opportunities, the size of our home, our
looks or body shape, whether we have children. Mothers of young
children go through periods when the most basic choices—when to
eat, sleep or go to the bathroom—are determined by someone else's
schedule and needs! Single women who may long to be at home raising children find themselves climbing a corporate ladder they would
rather leave behind.

Most of us must deal at some point with situations that narrow our
range of options, such as a dead-end job, a difficult marriage, demanding toddlers or singleness. How does one experience spiritual
transformation even when our outward circumstances are not what
we would choose? What are our choices when we feel we have none?

IN SEARCH OF FREEDOM

"Where the Spirit of the Lord is, there is freedom," Paul says (2 Corinthians 3:17). Indeed the whole spiritual journey could be characterized as a journey into freedom. That doesn't mean merely the physical freedom to come and go as we wish or the freedoms we
experience as citizens of a free country. For Paul, these kinds of freedoms came and went. Here Paul is talking about an interior freedom.
It is the freedom to be completely given over to God and to others in
love in any given moment. It is the ability to live from an inner secu-

rity, freed from self-interest, self-consciousness and self-protection. This is the freedom to live a life of utter responsiveness to the Spirit of God within us and among us rather than being limited or driven by the expectations of others. When we are living in this kind of freedom, we are no longer defined by our vulnerabilities and weaknesses, but at the same time we are willing to bless others through our vulnerability and weakness in this world. This freedom moves us from the perfectionism that binds to the grace of embracing what is most authentic within us and offering it freely to our world. This is the path of spiritual transformation in Christ.

[INTERIOR FREEDOM] IS THE FREEDOM TO BE COMPLETELY GIVEN OVER TO GOD AND TO OTHERS IN LOVE IN ANY GIVEN MOMENT.

To be honest, this has not generally been my experience. In my early thirties I began to acknowledge a growing awareness that I was not free in all the ways I wanted to be free. There were places in my life where I was in bondage—to expectations and limitations (real and perceived) placed on me by others, to my own inner compulsions and to popular misconceptions of what life in Christ is all about. I was ambushed by questions about what it meant to be a woman, what it meant to be a *Christian* woman, and what it meant to be surprised by a strength and passion within me that didn't seem to fit existing categories.

As disturbing as it was to start being more honest about such questions, there came a point where I realized that it was time for me to stop fighting the questions and instead allow them to start leading me into deeper levels to truth. "You will know the truth, and the truth will make you free," Jesus said (John 8:32). I was ready to see if that was really true.

At first it was exhilarating to give myself the freedom to ask new questions, make bold statements, take brave steps. But when the initial euphoria wore off and the journey began to take me to unknown places, it became a bit riskier than I had imagined. All of a sudden I had more responsibilities. I was stretched to the limits of my competencies and gifts, spirituality and wisdom. I found I was worried about different things. I worried about my children and how my choices were affecting them. I worried about myself and the pace I was keeping. I wondered whether I was adequate for all God was calling me to. It felt a little bit like the Israelites' grand exodus from Egypt. It was easy to be brave in the beginning, excited as they were about following God in new directions and leaving their bondage behind. But once they got a little farther from home and were truly on their own, they began to realize the enormity of the choice they had made and the new levels of responsibility that were associated with greater freedom. It was all so daunting that they started to question the wisdom of the whole thing. I know the feeling! The only thing that kept me going was my longing for freedom to follow God more fully and my growing awareness that the movement toward freedom is indeed the heart of the spiritual journey.

THE PATH TO SPIRITUAL TRANSFORMATION

The road to the kind of transformation we are talking about here is paved with truth—the truth about where we are now, the truth about where we want to go, and the truth about what it's going to take to walk out of bondage and into freedom. When the children of Israel embarked on their journey to Promised Land, they first had to face their bondage with greater realism. For a significant stretch of time, they had been unaware of the extent of their bondage. Perhaps they had even thought that living under someone else's rule was somehow normal or that it was the only option they had.

But eventually they could not avoid the truth of their situation. The pain and discomfort associated with living in bondage became harder to ignore. They needed someone to speak to them about the possibilities of living another way and help them to envision what it would look like to be more free. While being in bondage did offer some level of safety, security and familiarity, the call to freedom required them to take risks, to leave some things behind and move into unknown territory. They needed to believe in the possibility of a new way of being and desire it enough to risk moving from the known into the unknown. This is the journey for us as well.

The road to transformation always seems to lead us through the wilderness—that solitary place where the chaos in our soul starts to settle and it gets so quiet that we can finally hear the still small voice of God with clarity. Here in the wilderness, we are invited bit by bit to lay aside the stuff of our lives and parts of ourselves that at one time seemed essential. Now we can see that they only get in the way of the journey that God has for us. Clinging to what is old and comfortable only makes it harder to receive what is being given.

ON A PERSONAL NOTE

This book is largely an offering of discoveries claimed in the wilderness of my own questions and empty places—which is where most real change takes place. Just I was beginning to grapple with new questions, I was also being guided into the spiritual disciplines of solitude and silence, spiritual reading, spiritual direction and spiritual friendship. These disciplines were absolutely necessary, because they were the means by which I could give God access to the deeper places of my soul at a time when I needed to hear from God more than from anyone else. They gave me a way to listen, and they created quiet spaces within which God could speak. These practices sustained me and continue to sustain me in the wilderness places of my journey and beyond.

As a way of engaging the themes in this book more deeply, I invite you consider establishing a rhythm of spiritual practices similar to the rhythm that anchored me during this time of intense learning and transformation. I encourage you to commit yourself to the disciplines of solitude and silence, spiritual reading, prayer and journaling, and spiritual friendship as you read this book. At the end of each chapter there are spiritual exercises that guide you into these disciplines and create a context in which you too can listen to the issues and questions God is stirring up within your heart.

If you are one of those who can't put a book down once you've started it, go ahead and read the book through to get an overview. But make the commitment to go back and read it a second time more slowly, engaging in the spiritual practices and allowing God to speak deeply into your life.

IN SOLITUDE

Solitude is the time we set apart to give God our undivided attention. (I write about the disciplines of solitude and silence more fully in *Invitation to Solitude and Silence*, InterVarsity Press.) Consider establishing regular time for solitude—a half-hour to one hour would be optimal—and to read *Longing for More* in the context of your solitude times. Here are some thoughts on how you might do this.

Begin with silence. Before you begin reading the book, spend ten minutes in silence for the purpose of quieting yourself, becoming consciously aware of God's presence with you, and experiencing your own desire and willingness to hear from God. You might want to repeat the prayer from 1 Samuel 3:9: "Speak, LORD, for your servant is listening."

Spiritual reading. "Spiritual reading" refers to the nature and intent of our reading—our intent being not merely to gain information but to deepen our relationship with God by allowing him to speak to us directly through what we read. As you read *Longing for More,* listen for God's word to you in the moment. Be willing to notice your inner dynamics in response to what you hear. In spiritual reading it is helpful to pay particular attention to your experiences of *resonance* (a strong, gut-level sense that something is deeply true and speaks directly to your life) and *resistance* (those places where you disagree, have an uncomfortable emotional reaction, or want to argue with or resist the message of the text). You might even want to use two different highlighters as you read—one color to highlight places of resonance and one to highlight places of resistance—so that you can go back at the end of your time of reading and reflect on your reactions and response.

You can also allow your reading of *Longing for More* to guide you into dwelling on pertinent Scriptures as another way of receiving God's communication to you. Every chapter contains references to Scripture verses and biblical narratives. As God uses different Scriptures and stories in your life, live in them for as long as God is speaking to you through them—a day, a week, a month. The journey of spiritual freedom and transformation cannot be hurried.

Reflection. After reading each chapter, you will be invited to be silent for the purpose of deeper reflection on what you have read. I offer several questions that may be helpful to reflect on as you sit in silence. You may find that one particular question stands out as an item for deeper reflection during those moments. Or at the end of some chapters you may decide that it would be best not to think about a particular question at all but to just sit in silence and allow your mind to become still.

Prayer and journaling. Read slowly enough and in small enough portions that you have time to reflect on what you have read and to write your reflections in a journal or notebook. Use your journal to record feelings, thoughts and questions raised by the text. Especially note those places where it seems God is speaking to you and listen for what you would like to say to him in response. Allow your journal to become a record of your prayers.

You will find several questions relevant to the text under this section of the spiritual exercises as well. Again, don't feel that you need to answer every question. Read through the questions in the same way you read the text, looking for places of resonance or resistance. Listening to your gut-level reactions to the questions may help you discern which ones to focus on. You may find that just one or two questions spark something in you or lead you to something you would like to journal or pray about.

Invitations. At the end of each chapter (or at the end of each day's reading) ask, "Is there anything that God seems to be inviting me to do as a result of what I have read today?"

How will I respond to this invitation? You will find a brief prayer in this section of the spiritual exercises. You may want to use it to begin your own time of prayer and response. Do not feel that every reading has to lead into a major invitation. Just make it a point to ask, giving God the opportunity to speak to you in that way if he wishes. Sometimes his invitation may be as simple as "Just keep trusting me" or "Just stay with the process. You're doing great."

In Spiritual Friendship

The spiritual journey is not meant to be taken alone. Spiritual friendship is a relationship devoted to paying attention to the invitations of God in our lives and supporting one another in making a faithful response. Spiritual friends also check in with each other about our spiritual practices to see if we are engaging them in a way that meets our heart's deepest desire for God.

As you begin reading *Longing for More*, ask God to help you identify one or more individuals with whom you can share the experiences of seeking God and responding to his activity and initiative. Commit yourselves to pray for one another and call out the best in one another as you seek to respond courageously to God's invitations to you. This can be one other friend or a group of friends committed to taking the journey together. Each chapter includes guidance for sharing among spiritual friends, and appendix B provides discussion questions for use with others.

Even though the process of spiritual transformation is challenging, it is worth the cost—even when the cost seems exorbitant. It is my prayer that you will find here a safe place for listening to God's invitations to you, invitations that are contained within your own deep longing. There are desires in your heart that God is longing to meet. *"Trust in the LORD . . . delight in the LORD, and he will give you the desires of your heart"* (Psalm 37:3-4).

Spiritual Exercises

Alone with God

Silence. Take a few moments to sit with God in the silence of your heart. In the silence, reflect on these questions. Don't feel like you have to do anything. Just sit with the questions and with whatever comes.

- In what area of your life right now are you experiencing a longing for deeper levels of spiritual transformation?

- What are the choice points in your life where you are sensing the need to distinguish the True Voice from all the other voices that clamor for your attention?

Prayer and journaling. Review the chapter that you have just read, noticing the places of resonance and resistance that you highlighted. In your journal, tell God about your thoughts, feelings and questions, and then listen for his response.

- Where do the emotions and concerns expressed by other women mirror your own?

- Where did you find yourself saying, "That's exactly how I feel!" (resonance)?

- Where did you sense your own longing and frustration (resistance)?

- What does God seem to be saying to you in the midst of your questions and desires regarding the choices you're facing?

Invitations. "God, what are you saying to me through this reading? Are you inviting me to respond in some way?"

CHAPTER ONE

Finding Our Identity in Christ

Woman must come of age by herself—she must find her true
center alone.

ANNE MORROW LINDBERGH, *GIFT FROM THE SEA*

When I was in my late twenties, both of my grandfathers died within a few months of each other, each leaving behind a wife of more than fifty years. As a young wife and mother, I watched each of my grandmothers approach a casket to gaze at her husband's beloved body one last time. There was something oddly comforting about having each of those bodies present with us in the room for a little while longer, for they had housed precious souls, enabling them to be touched and known and loved in this life. Just before the casket was closed in that final parting of the ways, my Grandma Haley turned to my dad, her eldest son, and asked a poignant question: "How do you say goodbye?"

That is a good question, isn't it? As I watched my grandmothers struggling to say goodbye, I faced a reality that I had not yet been willing to face: our ultimate separateness from one another as human beings, even from those we love the most. In that moment the truth struck me: in one sense *we are all single!* Married or not, we all stand alone before God, accountable to him and to him alone for the expenditure of our life and love and spiritual service. Even those of us who do get married are single before marriage, after marriage or between marriages. And if the statistics hold true (on average, women live fifteen years longer than men do), most of us will find ourselves approaching the casket one day, struggling to say our own goodbye.

These moments at my grandfathers' funerals were not moments of morbid fatalism; rather, they were moments of clarity about the beauty and the limits of human relationship. No matter how greatly we have loved or how deeply we have committed ourselves, such partings of the way will come, sometimes due to death but at other times due to change, human frailty or betrayal. If our ability to survive in this world or if our sense of identity, self-worth, purpose and value is derived from the person whose body is in the casket, then the limits of human relationships seem all the more devastating.

Against this backdrop of life and death, change and humanness, Jesus' offer to be the primary and permanent source that fills our deepest needs becomes all the more precious. He offers to be the One who brings love and meaning to our life as we walk the road from our most open-hearted hellos to our most difficult goodbyes, with everything that comes in between. Our ultimate human separateness points us to a deeper truth: *none of us—married or single—can afford to invest our human relationships and endeavors with the meaning that only a relationship with God can provide.*

As a young woman, Anne Morrow Lindbergh captured this truth in her own words when she said,

> I want first of all to be at peace with myself. I want a singleness of eye, a purity of intention, a central core to my life to help me carry out these activities and obligations as well as I can. I want,

in fact, to live "in grace" as much of the time as possible. By grace I mean an inner harmony, essentially spiritual, which can be translated into outward harmony. I would like to achieve a state of inner spiritual grace from which I could function and give as I was meant to in the eyes of God.

As a result of her husband's death in 1975, Lindbergh faced in a fresh way what she called "woman's recurring lesson . . . 'woman must come of age by herself—she must find her true center alone.' The lesson seems to need relearning about every twenty years in a woman's life."

So how is it that we as women—married or single—can find all we need in Christ, so that our human relationships are sources of joy but do not take God's place? How do we learn to receive from God what only God can ultimately give?

LOOKING FOR LOVE IN ALL THE RIGHT PLACES

The truth is that women, for a variety of reasons and in a variety of ways, tend to look for love and a sense of self in many of the wrong places. Some of this has to do with fallen human nature, some with the ways women are socialized in our culture, and some with our psychological response to these experiences. Becoming willing to see these tendencies for what they are gives us an opportunity to move beyond them to the place where our relationship with Christ becomes the bedrock of our self-esteem.

Learning to find all we need in Christ begins with understanding how much he loves and values us. For some of us this is easier said than done. The experience of being female in contemporary culture is cause for severe depression for many woman—perhaps as many as one in four. In a comprehensive work on women and self-esteem, authors Linda Tscirhart Sanford and Mary Ellen Donovan observe, "Studies of women have repeatedly shown disturbing patterns: lack of self-esteem, an inability to feel powerful or in control of one's life, a vulnerability to depression, a tendency to see oneself as less talented, less able than one really is . . . a sense of being somehow not quite as good, not quite as able, not quite as bright, not quite as valuable as men. . . . when you leaf through the studies you can sense, floating in the air, ghosts of unborn dreams, unrealized hopes, undiscovered talents."

While women and men share basic human needs for identity and self-worth, there is much evidence that for women these commodities, which are crucial to living a full and functional life, can be very hard to come by. Unless a woman has been extraordinarily sheltered, her experiences in the family, the church, educational institutions, the business world, government, health-care institutions and the general public systematically rob her of the essentials of self-esteem.

Consider these common female experiences:

- A woman applies for admission to a Ph.D. program in computer science at a major university. Her qualifications (such as Graduate Record Exam score and grade-point average) are far superior to those of two men who apply at the same time. But they are admitted and she is not. The professors tell her they do not want to waste their time on a woman because she is likely to "get married and have children." (This really did happen—in 1992!)

- A single woman who is vice president in charge of finance and accounting in her professional life finds that instead of being included in a broad range of social and ministry opportunities in her church, she is relegated to "singles activities" reminiscent of the high school youth group. Meanwhile, her male counterparts are recruited for all manner of teaching and leadership roles. She wonders if she will ever be viewed as a full-fledged adult this side of marriage.

- A young mother spends all her waking hours knee-deep in diapers and dishes, wondering if she has any capacity left for intelligent thinking or adult conversation. On occasion she does accompany her husband to a business function, where her worst fears are confirmed. Once her husband's associates find out she is an at-home mom, they lose interest and focus almost exclusively on her husband.

- Many women attend church year after year and never hear significant teaching or messages given by other women. More than a few begin to wonder, *Don't women have anything to say that would be valuable to the congregation?*

- A woman works for her company for twelve years in a secretarial-type position that pays $18,000 a year. Despite her repeated requests to move into a sales position that would pay considerably more, her boss (who makes $150,000 a year) tells her, "No, we need you where you are now."

- A woman who has been thin all her life finds that she cannot lose the weight she gained during pregnancy. She avoids mirrors most of the time, but when she does happen to see herself, she can't help comparing herself unfavorably with images of the perfect women she sees in magazines and on television. To make matters worse, her husband often comments on the attractiveness of women he sees and muses out loud, "I wonder how she keeps herself in such good shape."

- A woman who has chosen to stay at home to raise her children rather than taking a paid job finds that she cannot get a credit card, apply for a mortgage or buy a car without her husband's signature. When her husband dies, she realizes how dependent and vulnerable she has become.

- Over the years, a woman puts her husband through graduate school, works beside him to start a business, manages the home and raises the children, accompanies him to business functions and gives numerous dinner parties. She looks forward to a time when she and her husband can relax, travel together and enjoy the fruit of their labors. Instead, just as their youngest child is preparing to leave for college, her husband leaves her for a younger woman. Rather than enjoying some long-awaited companionship in her middle years, she finds herself shattered and alone.

- A forty-three-year-old single woman sees single men her age celebrated as "eligible bachelors" while she is considered an "old maid."

These are *not* isolated incidents. Each one is a real-life experience relived over and over again by real women in the United States. In many countries the situation for women is even worse. A 1994 cover article in *U.S News & World Report* titled "The War Against Women" documented how women are being used and abused in country after country. In fact, according to the 1993 United Nations Human Development Report, "There is still no country that treats its women as well as its men." The statement is validated with painful descriptions of the hiring and firing of women on the basis of their sex appeal, the aborting and poisoning of girl babies, genital mutilation of young girls, the punishment of rape victims, domestic "accidents" and murders that take place when a young wife doesn't please her husband, and across-the-board discrimination in jobs and compensation.

FACING OUR OLDEST ENEMY

What is the impact on a woman's self-esteem when she takes an honest look at these facts?

For starters, we can begin to understand that the problem we have with knowing who we are and what we are worth is rooted in systems much older and larger than ourselves. Beliefs about women have been shaped by ideas, principles, rules and procedures that have long governed the world. Significant—and seemingly insignificant—events whisper to us day in and day out, "See, you are not quite as good as _____, you don't matter quite as much." Even those of us with few experiences of personal suffering are not untouched by the demeaning experiences of women struggling for the essentials of self-esteem and worth here and in other countries. The pain of being put down and having to fight for basic human rights as a population group is a part of our "collective consciousness" as women. We may be shocked by articles such as the one from *U.S News & World Report,* but the fact is, many women are so used to being seen and treated as "less than" that it is hard to distinguish discrimination from other hard experiences.

Whether the abuse and disrespect of women is overt or more subtle, the universality of the female experience of being "less than" is astounding. When we delve into the experiences of women across barriers of race and time, we can see that women's extraordinary deprivation of dignity, equality and worth is not only systemic but a direct result of the enmity that came between Satan and the woman in the Garden of Eden so long ago (Genesis 3:15). Ever since that day, women have been particular targets of Satan for all manner of discrimination, abuse and inhumane treatment. Shame, blame and domination, introduced as a result of sin, became tools of Satan to destroy the human family by causing one grouping of people to set themselves up as better than another—men over women, one ethnic group over another, one religious group over another.

Women's fight to gain equality and a sense of worth is not a product of the feminist movement or some "liberal" theology. It is a battle that has been raging throughout human history. When we seek to restore to women (or anyone else who has been discriminated against) the dignity and equality that God intended when he created us, we are, in a very real sense, engaged in battle against Satan himself, who is still active in human affairs. We echo Old and New Testament prophets alike when we recognize and denounce the invisible systems that govern our world. "Our struggle is not against enemies of blood and flesh, but against the rulers, against the authorities, against the cosmic powers of this present darkness, against the spiritual forces of evil in the heavenly places" (Ephesians 6:12).

The High Cost of Low Self-Esteem

Kari Torjesen Malcolm, who grew up as a missionary kid in China, has seen the ramifications of low self-esteem in her own life. When Kari moved to the United States from China as an adult, she made herself sick trying to fit in with popular Western ideas about what a woman could and should be. Although Kari had a strong and effective witness to students on the secular college campus where she was teaching, some of her associates in the Christian organization with which she was affiliated thought she should give up her teaching post when it came time for her to get married. Not wishing to be divisive, Kari did just that. But her heartbreak at having left her teaching job and the deep friendships with her students caused tension during the early years of her marriage.

I was beginning to listen to the common teaching that a woman's chief role is to be a support to her husband in his ministry, be a homemaker and raise children to follow the Lord. I was a woman at war with myself. While I tried to agree with my conscious mind to a view that limited a woman's contribution to the kingdom, my subconscious revolted within me. . . .

Overcome with grief over the ministry I had left and trying to fit into the role of a submissive homemaker, I felt myself losing my identity. Who was I? For the first time in my life, I developed the "I'm just a woman" syndrome. When I could no longer look at myself as a precious disciple and disciplemaker, a friend of Jesus Christ, I became sick. Many months were spent in bed with an undiagnosed fever. After the fever subsided, I went into a deep depression. Guilt feelings about having left my first love (Christ) swept over me—some from God and some based on false regret.

Many women do not move through life with the strength that comes from a sense of well-being, purpose and competence. Several key principles are important to recognizing and healing our wounded self-esteem.

Know how much you are worth. Jesus' conversation with the woman of Samaria in John 4 demonstrates that Christ brings all the elements of personhood that make for wholeness and abundant life to the sisters as well as the brothers in the family of God. First of all, he wants us to know how much we are worth.

Female children face a greater risk than male children of growing up with uncertainty and mixed messages about their worth. The Samaritan woman of John 4—we'll call her Samara, since her name is not given—had additional reasons to believe that she wasn't worth

much, that no one could possibly love her. Not only was she of the
lesser sex, she was also of a lesser race, and she was known for her
blatant immorality. She had had five husbands, and at the time she
met Christ, she was living with a man to whom she was not married.

It is not hard to imagine the disillusionment that Samara must
have carried with her as she came to Jacob's well on the day her path
crossed that of Christ. She must have experienced a range and intensity of emotion: anger, sadness and disillusionment, feelings of being
used and misunderstood. The fact that she chose to draw water in the
heat of the day rather than in the cool of the morning suggests that
she was so depressed and ostracized that she avoided contact with
those who might demean her. She was aware of how people viewed
her, so much so that she expressed surprise that Jesus would even ini-
tiate conversation with her: "How is it that you, a Jew, ask a drink of
me, a woman of Samaria?" (John 4:9).

But Christ demonstrated that there was no damaging favoritism
with him. Just by beginning an intelligent conversation with her and
treating her as an equal, Jesus communicated her significance. Most
men would not have been willing to risk their reputation by being
found in conversation with a woman such as this (in Jewish custom
it was considered inappropriate for a man to talk with his own wife
in public, let alone a "loose" woman). With a surprising lack of concern for appearances, Christ chose to walk right into Samaria and ini-
tiate a conversation with a woman who was "less than" in every way
that mattered to the people of that day.

Even so, Christ did not treat Samara as though she were beneath
him or needed to be pulled out of the gutter and saved. Instead, he
treated her as someone he could talk to on an equal level. In the
course of the conversation Jesus affirmed her intelligence and ability
to understand spiritual truth by discussing theology with her. He re-

vealed new truth that was (as far as we can tell) unknown to anyone else—including the disciples! When the disciples came to offer him lunch, he made it clear that talking with Samara was the most important thing he could be doing at the moment. The value that Christ placed on her was undiminished by his knowledge of her deepest, darkest secrets. What an amazing first this must have been for her, and how life changing it was!

Know who you are as an individual and as part of a community. Another key to a woman's self-esteem is knowledge of herself as an individual who is unique and separate from others, balanced by a sense of how she fits into her community. Many women lack self-esteem precisely because they know little about themselves. Doing research on self-esteem, Linda Tschirhart Sanford and Mary Ellen Donovan discovered that there are real reasons that many women have little sense of themselves as fully developed individuals in the midst of a larger whole: "Many women we interviewed had great difficulty describing themselves at all. 'Shot full of holes,' 'full of gaps,' 'blank—not much self there,' are just some of the phrases these women used to describe themselves. A woman who sees herself as a blank has virtually no chance of experiencing self-esteem."

Many women focus so much on pleasing other people that they are out of touch with their own desires and needs. A married woman may feel that her purpose in life is only to support her husband in the priorities of his life or to help her children find their niche—rather than finding one of her own where *both* husband and wife are encouraged and supported in finding their niches. She may be lulled into a false sense of security because she has a man to take care of her, naively believing that she has no need of any skills besides those associated with housekeeping and childcare. Or a woman may be accustomed to accepting the values of her parents or pastor without ever asking her own hard questions and searching out God's answers for herself.

This sense of "blankness," of lost identity, perhaps is most evident when we let ourselves be defined by whether we have a man. For instance, a single woman may feel she can't have a full identity without a husband, so she waits to pursue her interests and develop her gifts until she is married and "real life" begins. Samara is a striking example of this; it is safe to say that she had very little sense of herself apart from her continued attempts to find the right man. Women who are married may attach their identity entirely to their husband.

As I have worked with girls and women in many different settings, I have known women who dropped out of school to follow a man around, women who rushed into marriage with the wrong man just so they wouldn't be alone, women who gave in to sexual pressure out of fear of losing a man, women who were so tied to the home and to their man's schedule that they were not even free to go out for lunch with a friend, women who lived so completely for their man that they wouldn't consider inconveniencing him by taking a class or a part-time job that would keep them challenged and growing.

I know women who have spent a lifetime adapting to their husband's life and calling—enduring financial hardship so he can go to school, holding down the fort at home while he travels, managing the household while he spends long hours working, studying or ministering, being tolerant of the stress all of this places on the marriage and family—never thinking of asking for the same opportunities for themselves. Somehow they feel that the privilege of having that kind of support in life goes with being male, not female.

How has this happened? Why do we think we are worth so little that we allow our identity to be overshadowed by others'? Mary Stewart Van Leeuwen draws our attention to God's warning in Genesis 3:16 that men and women, in their distinct ways, would have a tendency to misuse the dominion and "one-fleshness" that was built into humanity at creation. Just as men have a tendency to twist responsible dominion into wrongful domination, the peculiarly female sin is to preserve relationships at all costs—even if the cost is her own lack of responsible action in the world.

Yes, men and women were created to be together and flourish in loving relationships. However, even though we may be looking forward to or are presently enjoying a relationship with a man, *we cannot let our love and desire for a man overshadow our love and commitment to serving God as fully developed human beings.* If I live for my husband and adapt to him in such a way that I do not live for God my Creator and Jesus my Savior and Lord, I am committing the sin of idolatry— I am giving something else a higher priority than I give God.

We also have misdirected priorities when we allow others to define us rather than finding our identity in Christ. We often identify ourselves by our career, our achievements, our sex appeal or the roles we play (such as "mom" or "the single daughter"). All these forms of identity have been society's way, at one time or another, of defining us as women. The problem is that these aspects of life are changeable and temporary. Any woman who has lost a job, who has gone through the aging process or whose marital status has changed would attest to that. As important as these parts of life are at different times, they are inadequate as a way of defining ourselves.

The sure foundation of self-esteem is the knowledge that before, during and after life with a husband, children, a career or even a youthful and physically able body, we are created to reflect God's character, to love him and have honest, intimate communication with him. God's purposes for our lives include our roles as wives, daughters, mothers and career women, but go beyond those identities. Our identity is rooted in God's unconditional love for us. He has given us gifts and resources to make a unique contribution to our world for his glory. We work in partnership with him as we receive with a grateful heart the gifts he has given us, develop them and use them to contribute positively to this world. We honor him as we become all he created us to be, reaching out in love and service to our physical family, our spiritual family and community, and the larger human family to which we belong.

When Samara met Christ, he made it clear that it was not her relationship with a man that defined her. He encouraged a realistic self-assessment when he gave her the opportunity to face her sin and her failure to relate in a healthy fashion with men (John 4:16-17). But Christ was quick to point out the true source of her identity: "It's who you are and the way you live that count before God. Your worship must engage your spirit in the pursuit of truth. That's the kind of people the Father is out looking for: those who are simply and honestly *themselves* before him in their worship" (John 4:23 *The Message*).

No longer would Samara be defined by gender, race, marital status or desirability to men. Once she placed her faith in Jesus, realizing that he was the Messiah for whom she had been waiting (John 4:29), she received a spiritual identity that transcended all other roles and relationships. She, along with all of us who have put our faith in Christ, "are the ones chosen by God, chosen for the high calling of priestly work, chosen to be a holy people, God's instruments to do his work and speak out for him, to tell others of the night-and-day difference he made for you—from nothing to something, from rejected to accepted" (1 Peter 2:9-10 *The Message*).

These and many other Scriptures define Christian women and men first and foremost in terms of their priestly function. We dare not lay down our true identity for any human being or system that would seek to define us as anything less than full-fledged priests and disciples. If we do, we will be very empty indeed. The challenge for women today is to take responsibility for the adult task of defining ourselves, not in relation to gender roles, career or sex appeal but in relation to the identity, worth, purpose and enabling that come from God himself. (For further discussion of this subject, see chapter four.)

UNDERSTAND GOD'S PURPOSES FOR YOUR LIFE

In relating with Samara, Christ provided her with yet another essential of self-esteem: the opportunity to live purposefully and have an impact.

When the disciples returned from town with lunch, "they were astonished that [Jesus] was speaking with a woman" (John 4:27). Rather than expressing their shock out loud, they stood there gaping until Samara hurried away—probably, in part, to escape their curious stares.

Knowing their thoughts, Jesus began to point out that they were right in the middle of a community that was ripe for responding to the message of the true Messiah. Indeed, while they sat there talking about the possibilities, Samara was already in town, getting the job done. With great urgency she had hurried back to the city and was telling everyone she knew, "Come and see a man who told me everything I have ever done! He cannot be the Messiah, can he?" (John 4:29).

And the people came! Because of Samara's witness, many of the Samaritans in that place believed in Christ. They asked him to stay a little longer, so Jesus stayed two more days, giving many more people a chance to hear him speak and to entrust their lives to him. By the time he left they were able to say to Samara, "It is no longer because of what you said that we believe, for we have heard for ourselves, and we know that this is truly the Savior of the world" (John 4:42). She had instigated a major evangelistic campaign because she had been called and enabled by God himself.

This part of Samara's story is thrilling because it speaks to our own deep longings to accomplish something meaningful and lasting with our lives. "We have been made with a capacity to move purposefully in a direction, to join God in his purposes. We are far more than senseless parts of a preordered system that fatalistically moves us along. Therefore, in our innermost being, we thirst to be a part of the eternal plan, to make a lasting difference in our world. *We long for impact.*"

Christ knew that Samara needed more meaning for her life than stereotypical "women's work" and chasing after men. And so that is what he brought her. He didn't wait for Samara to work out the right marital status, to be discipled, to join a church or to get an education. He walked into Samaria that day and chose a woman right where she was in life to bring a whole community to himself. How refreshing!

Samara's story has motivated me over the years to open myself to the possibilities of purposeful living—even those purposes that to others seem inappropriate or out of the ordinary. The process of learning to live according to God's purposes is so rewarding, so meaningful and so crucial that I have devoted the next chapter to it.

DEVELOP SKILLS FOR FUNCTIONING IN THE REAL WORLD

Closely connected with the need to know that our lives have purpose is our need for competence—having the skills necessary to survive, thrive and accomplish God's purposes. The need for competence presents another very real challenge for women in our society.

This is not to say that women should abandon competency in areas of home and family. Men and women alike need to take seriously the responsibility of developing skills and competencies to maintain a home. However, women in our society have not always been encouraged to achieve outside the home or to be independent. This is another detriment to healthy self-esteem. All women need to develop the confidence that comes from knowing that their skills are valuable in society and that they have the ability and know-how to provide for themselves and their children, should they be called upon to do so.

Often a woman becomes aware of gaps in her self-esteem and personal identity around the time she begins thinking about what she is going to do once her children are in school, off at college or married. At this time in a family's life, more income may be needed because of college bills, weddings and other expenses, so it is decided that the woman will go back to work. (The need to be able to generate income comes even sooner for a woman whose circumstances change due to divorce, her husband's death or her husband's unemployment—eventualities to which none of us are immune.) If she has not finished her education or has let her credentials and marketable experience lapse, she may find that her options are limited to low-paying jobs outside her fields of interest and abilities. Thus, she might miss out on the sense of self-worth that comes from developing her interests and gifts, and using them in the context of work that is meaningful and challenging. In many cases, she faces this situation while her husband is enjoying the satisfaction and challenge of a well-established career in his chosen field.

Whether we choose to stay home full time and raise children or work outside the home or some combination of both, the time comes when all of us find ourselves in the middle of this life transition. We do well to be aware that it is coming and to prepare for it by continuing to maintain and develop the skills that will enable us to navigate the transition and care for ourselves in ways that correspond to our gifts and interests.

A single woman may confront similar challenges if she chooses not to invest in her career or fully develop her skills because she assumes that when she gets married her husband will support her. In reality she may or may not get married, and if she does, her husband's income may or may not fully care for the family's financial needs. A woman who has not married may experience a sense of hopelessness about herself and her future even though she has many gifts and great potential for developing them.

Given high divorce rates and women's tendency to significantly outlive their husbands, the truth is that in the United States and many other parts of the world, *the woman who cannot support herself is either an actual or potential victim of financial stress and poverty.* Thus, whether she is married or single, it is crucial for a woman to broaden her range of skills so that she can support herself with meaningful work—not only for her self-esteem but also for the provision of physical necessities.

Men can work with women to ensure that they receive the same kind of support that they themselves expect for their career and ministry goals. This does not mean that family priorities have to fly out the window, as I will discuss more fully in chapter nine. Particularly if she has the support of a loving husband, a woman can remain committed to her family and still carve out some time for further schooling, job experiences that keep her skills current and her foot in the door of a meaningful career or ministry, or volunteer work that will contribute to a well-rounded resumé.

For myself, working out a balance between being available to my family and continuing to develop vocationally has been crucial to self-esteem. There is a feeling of well-being that comes from knowing that I am doing what is right for my family and that I haven't missed out on being an integral part of their lives. But I also need to know that the part of me that stands before God alone and fits into his larger plan is continuing to develop and grow. It is satisfying to know that I am generating income our family needs, but doing it in ways that I enjoy and that reflect God's calling on my life. Because of the commitment my husband, Chris, and I share to continue investing in these aspects of my life, I do not have inordinate fears about future possibilities—something happening to Chris or his job, or our children leaving the nest. Rather, I feel confidence and enthusiasm about the future, knowing that God's purposes for me will always remain and I have been prepared for them. Women who value themselves—and the men who value them—will insist on this essential element of self-esteem, recognizing that self-esteem is not just a feeling, it is a result of practical actions.

GAIN REALISTIC INFORMATION ABOUT HOW THE WORLD WORKS

We women also need to understand how the world outside our homes functions. The world is made up of different systems—your own family system (or way of doing things), the legal system, welfare, educational and religious systems, and others. Each system has its own processes, communication patterns, relational webs and ways of getting things done, as well as its own vulnerabilities and dysfunctions. People who know how to work within these systems will be better off in them.

Women are sometimes naive, uninformed or inexperienced regarding how to "work" systems, and this leaves us very vulnerable within them. We lack information about how to protect ourselves from being taken advantage of, how to use the legal system, how to buy and take care of a car, how to invest money and plan for a financial future, how to understand the fine print on documents we sign—

and the list goes on. Learning about the systems we participate in and rely on for our practical needs is another very important way of increasing our sense of well-being and confidence in the world.

There is a fine line, however, between participating in a system in ways that are healthy and for the good of all and "working the system" in dishonest, selfish or manipulative ways. This is where we rely on ethics and values. A clear sense of what is right and wrong and what matters most in life will determine how we use the information and skills we have. A person who has a strong moral ethic will work within the system in ways that are honest. She will be complimentary when she honestly has something good to say but will refuse to flatter for the sake of getting ahead. To the best of her ability she will tell the truth even when the truth is unpopular, but she will know how to pick her time and place. A woman who values all people will use her knowledge of how the world works not only for her own good but also for the good of others. The Bible calls this being "as shrewd as snakes and as innocent as doves" (Matthew 10:16 NIV).

At times a woman may realize that a system in which she has been participating stands for something contrary to her ethics or values. She may begin to see that in a particular system, women or people of color are discriminated against, dishonesty is required in order to get ahead, or people are manipulated and used. In this case her ethics and values will guide her to take a stand or to leave the system altogether.

A certain confidence comes from knowing that we are increasing our understanding of the world, that we are not depending on someone else to do "the hard stuff" for us, and that even in the difficult and sometimes confusing dilemmas we face, we are hammering out a set of ethics and values that are grounded in God's Word. Without these abilities, without this foundation of ethics and values to guide us, we will tend to live timidly, full of uncertainty, afraid to make a move.

THE LESSON OF A LIFETIME

Samara found herself loved in brand-new ways the day she met Christ at the well. But the ultimate expression of his love—his willingness to lay down his life in payment for our sin—was still in the future. We have seen Christ's love for us in ways that Samara did not have the opportunity to see. We know that if any one of us had been the *only* one needing salvation from sin, Jesus still would have given his all. But that is only the beginning.

Each of us needs to cultivate our relationship with Christ as if it were only the two of us, because chances are a time will come when this is the case. That is why exploring this love relationship is so important—so that we can begin to see ourselves as God sees us and root our self-esteem in the bedrock of his love.

One woman has written down brief statements that reflect what she has learned about God's view of her, and she repeats them to herself daily:

- I am complete in Christ.
- I am a worthwhile person just as I am.
- I stand alone before God as a whole person.
- I have talents and abilities that God gives because he expresses himself through me.
- I can love others and give good things to them because God's love is poured out in my heart.
- I have self-esteem and integrity on my own because I am just as God intended me to be.

You might want to record your our own discoveries about God's love for you as you ponder the Scriptures (his love letter to you) and listen attentively to his voice as he speaks love to you in the midst of

your ordinary days. Many experiences can drag us into the pit of feeling "less than" if we don't have truth with which to respond.

In addition, past messages about our worth (or the lack of it) inform the way we view ourselves today. Family and religious systems
that were characterized by shame, sexism, abuse of women and children, conditional love based on performance, or an inability to express love contribute significantly to a woman's feeling of powerless-
ness and worthlessness. Christ, through the presence of the Holy
Spirit (the Helper or Counselor as he is called in John 14–16), will
walk with us as we sort through these early messages. We do not confront the past for the purpose of blaming others or making excuses
for ourselves; we explore past experiences and messages to uncover
the lies that are misleading us and to enter more fully into the truth.
Only then can we be free from self-absorption and self-deprecation
and give to God and others from the fullness he intends.

Of course we do not learn these lessons once and for all. There
have been and continue to be times when we all must come back to
the most basic of life's lessons, as I did at my grandfathers' funerals.
On such occasions we face the reality that even if we are married or
in other ways close to another human being, life is still a solitary journey. In these moments of awareness, I need to hear God say, "I will
never leave you or forsake you" (Hebrews 13:5). In times when people or circumstances seem limiting, I need to learn to come back to
God and ask, "Who are you calling me to be? What do you want me
to do?" When I fail and feel that my usefulness to God is over, I need
to listen as he says, "My love for you and your usefulness to me are
not conditional upon your performance. I didn't wait for perfection
from Samara before I gave her love and the chance to make a difference, and I'm not waiting for perfection from you."

Learning to find all we need in Christ is truly the lesson of a lifetime. It is tempting to oversimplify and overspiritualize the problem many of us have with self-esteem, thinking that if we just tell ourselves over and over again how much God loves us, pretty soon we will be convinced. As foundational as this knowledge is, many of the essentials of self-esteem (like understanding God's purposes for our lives, developing skills and competencies for functioning in the world, working from a clearly articulated set of values) are very practical in nature, as we have seen in this chapter. God knows about these practical needs as well as the spiritual ones, and we can ask him to provide these things. He can be trusted to lead us in acquiring what is essential at the right time and in the right way as we are open and responsive to his leading.

SPIRITUAL EXERCISES

Alone with God

Silence. As you come to the end of this chapter, take a few moments to sit with God in the silence of your heart and reflect on the following questions. Don't feel like you have to do anything. Just sit with the questions and with whatever comes up in you as you listen.

- During what moments do you experience the reality of your "singleness"—your ultimate separateness from other human beings?

- How do you feel in these moments?

- What questions does this awareness raise for you?

- What do you tend to do during these times when you are aware of this ultimate separateness? How is God present (or absent) during such times?

Prayer and journaling. Review the chapter that you have just read, noticing the places of resonance and resistance that you highlighted. In your journal, write and tell God about the thoughts, feelings, desires and questions that this chapter raised for you. Notice the places where you experienced emotion or grief about ways in which you are depending on others for what only God can give. Or perhaps there are places where you want to argue or express anger about the injustices women face and the ways those affect you. In your journal, go ahead and express your feelings as well as your arguments and places of disagreement.

- What does your reaction indicate about what is going on in the deep places of your soul?

- What does God seem to be saying to you in the midst of your emotions and questions?

Invitations. "God, how are you inviting me to respond to what you are saying to me through this reading?"

Saying Yes to God's Purposes

*I believe that what a woman resents is not so much giving herself in pieces
as giving herself purposelessly. . . . Purposeful giving is not as apt to deplete
one's resources; it belongs to that natural order of giving that seems to renew
itself even in the act of depletion. The more one gives, the more one has to
give—like milk in the breast.*

ANNE MORROW LINDBERGH, *GIFT FROM THE SEA*

"The hardest thing about being a homemaker," I have wailed on
many occasions, "is the repetitiveness of the tasks! Almost everything
I do in life has to be done over again within hours or days. It all seems
so pointless!"

My personal symbol of futility is the kitchen floor. It is a white
floor (I picked it out myself!) that is just beautiful when it is clean.
The problem, of course, is that no sooner have I cleaned it (usually
on my hands and knees after having planned my whole day around
it) than someone spills on it. I know that *never* is a very big word, but
this never fails.

The inevitability of it all has made this a family joke, and on my
good days I can laugh along. However, on my bad days I begin to
babble incoherently about the futility of my life: What does life mat-

ter when I spend my days doing things that have been undone by the time my husband gets home? What do I have to show for the exhaustion I feel at the end of the day? Why do I bother? It can go on and on. For sanity purposes, I have been known to wash the floor in the late afternoon and then insist that we all go out for dinner so that it stays clean for at least several hours. Anything for a sense of accomplishment!

Let's face it: with all the options open to women today, our lives are still often filled with the mundane, the ridiculous, the difficult, even the tragic. Sometimes it is hard to feel that life has purpose when you spend most of your days scraping Play-Doh off the floor, cleaning the bathroom or working for a boss who doesn't recognize your potential.

And yet all of us, deep down inside, harbor a very human desire for meaning in life. We want our life to count for something, something that will last longer than a few hours or a few days. As one poet put it: "Life without meaning is the torture of restlessness and vague desire. It is a boat longing for the sea and yet afraid." It is this longing and restlessness that God wants to fill with his purposes.

ESTHER: A WOMAN TRANSFORMED BY PURPOSE

Esther was a woman for whom the mundane and tragic aspects of life took on new meaning when she saw them in the context of God's purposes. As a result of this new understanding, she was utterly transformed from a frightened and somewhat passive woman into one of strength, courage and action.

Esther's story takes place in Persia (present-day Iran) during the reign of King Xerxes. The opening scene, described in Esther 1, reveals Xerxes treating all of his officials, noblemen and armies to a lavish banquet that was the culmination of a six-month period in which he had displayed the wealth and splendor of his kingdom. The royal wine flowed freely, and the men drank without restraint. At the same time his wife, Queen Vashti, gave a separate banquet for the women in another part of the palace.

At the end of this seven-day banquet, when Xerxes was "merry with wine" (in other words, he was drunk), he called Queen Vashti to come and display her beauty to his drunken guests. One can only imagine the state that the king and his male guests were in after drinking and partying for seven days straight. Some historians believe that the king was commanding Vashti to appear naked except for her crown, and most agree it was not a respectful request but a demeaning one. Certainly this was not the kind of situation in which any self-respecting woman would willingly place herself.

When Vashti refused to display herself as the king had commanded, the king's men convinced him that her behavior was a threat not only to his honor but also to male supremacy in general. He decided to make a public example of her by banishing her from his presence and giving her position to one who was more worthy. Women had few rights during this period; women were expendable and at the mercy of the men in their lives. It was into this setting that Esther came.

A beauty pageant with a twist. When the king's anger subsided, he began to miss Vashti. His attendants, who didn't want to risk losing all the progress they had made for mankind, came up with the idea of distracting Xerxes from what he was feeling by staging a beauty pageant! They gathered all the beautiful young virgins in the kingdom into a harem for the king so that he could choose a replacement for Vashti.

Esther, an orphaned Jewish girl in the care of her cousin Mordecai, was one of the young virgins who was captured for the harem. We don't know if she was shopping in the outdoor market, laughing with

friends or working around her home when the king's men rode
through town seizing beautiful girls. It is not hard to imagine her
panic and fright as she was torn from her family and taken against
her will to the king's palace. Who knows if she even realized, as she
was being dragged away, that she would spend the next full year getting ready for one night of sex with a heathen king.

Esther 2:12-14 tells us that there was considerably more involved
in the Miss Persia beauty pageant than in the pageants to which we are
accustomed. After the young woman was brought into the harem, she
spent twelve months getting ready—six months of beauty treatments
with oil and myrrh and six months with herbs and cosmetics. When
her turn came, she would spend the night with the king and then return to the second harem of the concubines. She was then considered
used merchandise, the equivalent of a slave kept for the purposes of
sex, childbearing and housekeeping. She could never approach the
king again unless he called her by name. Some beauty pageant!

If Esther was like most Jewish girls, she had dreamed all her life of
marrying and bearing children; perhaps she had even imagined that
she would be the one chosen to be the mother of the Messiah. But
now her prospects of a normal marriage and family life were ruined,
for she would become forever the property of the king. Here was the
trauma of kidnapping and rape, the loneliness of being torn from
family, the disappointment of a difficult marriage, and the loss of her
hopes and dreams—all wrapped up in one life-changing event. Mordecai couldn't do much beyond advising her not to tell anyone she
was a Jew. (Maybe he thought she would receive better treatment if
no one knew she belonged to the race that had once been held captive in that country.) But certainly his presence as he walked back and
forth in front of the harem every day must have been a comfort and
a strength to his young cousin.

Hope in the midst of tragedy. As dismal as Esther's situation was, God was there—in the harem, in the palace and in the king's bedroom—working in all of his sovereignty and power to bring about his good purposes. As Esther spent the next year preparing to go to the king, she found favor with everyone who knew her. And when her turn came, "the king loved Esther more than all the other women; of all the virgins she won his favor and devotion, so that he set the royal crown on her head and made her queen instead of Vashti" (Esther 2:17). Although she was not yet aware of it, the king's love would become the key to the accomplishment of God's great purpose in that place.

After Esther was settled in her new position as queen, King Xerxes promoted a proud and evil man named Haman to a position above all the other palace officials. The king then commanded that everyone should bow down to Haman. Mordecai, consistent with his Jewish faith and practice, refused. This refusal caused quite a stir: "When Haman saw that Mordecai did not bow down or do obeisance to him, Haman was infuriated. But he thought it beneath him to lay hands on Mordecai alone. So, having been told who Mordecai's people were, Haman plotted to destroy all the Jews, the people of Mordecai, throughout the whole kingdom of Ahasuerus [Xerxes]" (3:5-6).

Haman cleverly convinced the king that the Jews scattered throughout the country were a threat to his supremacy. So the king gave permission for Haman to send out this edict: on the thirteenth day of the twelfth month, the king's soldiers would be sent out into all the king's provinces to "destroy, to kill, and to annihilate all Jews, young and old, women and children, in one day . . . and to plunder their goods" (3:13).

When Mordecai got wind of Haman's genocidal plot against the Jews, he realized immediately the significance of Esther's position. He sent her a message urging her to "go to the king to make supplication to him and entreat him for her people" (4:8). At first Esther was hesitant to get involved, and with very good reason. She reminded Mordecai that "if any man or woman goes to the king inside the inner court without being called, there is but one law—all alike are to be put to death. Only if the king holds out the golden scepter to someone, may that person live. I myself have not been called to come in to the king for thirty days" (4:11).

At this point Mordecai, who must have been very wise, made an interesting suggestion. After expressing complete confidence in God's ability to deliver the Jews, he said to Esther, "Who knows? Perhaps you have come to royal dignity for just such a time as this" (4:14). He didn't presume to tell her what God was calling her to do; he merely heightened her awareness with his insightful question. God's call on our life is very personal and he alone must speak it to our soul.

As a result of Mordecai's comment, the light began to dawn for Esther regarding all that had happened to her. The trauma, the loneliness, the unusualness of her situation began to make sense. As she became conscious of what she had come to the kingdom for, a sense of purpose—not personal safety, probabilities, social norms or convenience—began to inform her decision-making process. The knowledge that God had brought her to this time and place for a specific purpose transformed her from a frightened, hesitant woman making excuses in Esther 4:11 to the courageous woman who sent this message to Mordecai: "Go, gather all the Jews . . . and hold a fast on my behalf. . . . I and my maids will also fast as you do. After that I will go to the king, though it is against the law; and if I perish, I perish" (4:16).

Following through. After asking the Jews to fast and pray for her, Esther took several days to think of a plan and prepare her heart. Then she swung into action. First, she made herself beautiful, the mundane task of getting dressed taking on a new significance that day. Can't you just see her standing in front of her closet, trying to choose the royal robe that would please the king and cause his heart to be open toward her? Perhaps her heart beat fast and her fingers shook as she applied her makeup. Maybe she rehearsed what she would say to the king if she did get the chance to speak. Certainly she thought of Queen Vashti in those moments, questioning whether she too would be banished for standing up for her convictions. She had spoken bravely three days earlier, but now the moment of truth had come. Would she have the courage to follow through?

Esther did follow through. She used everything at her disposal—her brains, her beauty, her position, the king's love for her—and risked it all to accomplish the purpose for which God had brought her to that time and place. She went and stood in the inner court of the king's palace, positioning herself so that the king could see her. She didn't have to wait long, for "as soon as the king saw Queen Esther standing in the court, she won his favor and he held out to her the golden scepter that was in his hand. Then Esther approached [the king]. . . . [He] said to her, 'What is it, Queen Esther? What is your request? It shall be given you, even to the half of my kingdom'" (5:2-3).

From there Esther implemented a wildly successful plan that resulted in Haman being hanged on the gallows he had built for Mordecai and the Jews being delivered from annihilation. Mordecai was promoted to a position of authority second only to the king himself and used his position for the good of his people, while Esther continued to enjoy the love of the king and the privileges and responsibilities of queenship. To this day the Jews celebrate the feast of Purim "as the days on which the Jews gained relief from their enemies, and as the month that had been turned for them from sorrow into gladness and from mourning into a holiday" (9:22). What a thrilling story of the mighty way God used a woman who had been uniquely prepared for his great purposes.

SEEING OURSELVES AS WOMEN OF PURPOSE

The sovereignty of God permeates the book of Esther. It was such an unlikely situation in human terms. But even so, Esther needed to consider the suggestion Mordecai raised for her that day. She had not yet begun to realize that God had been carefully orchestrating her life to bring her to that place at that time for that purpose. He had put together a package in her life—beauty, intelligence, nationality, position, love—and now the time had come for her to put it to use.

GOD IS PUTTING TOGETHER A PACKAGE IN EACH OF OUR LIVES, PREPARING US TO MAKE A UNIQUE CONTRIBUTION TO HIS KINGDOM. WE NEED TO ASK OURSELVES, *WHAT HAVE I COME TO THE KINGDOM FOR? WHY HAS GOD BROUGHT ME TO THIS PARTICULAR TIME AND PLACE?*

The sovereignty of God permeates our lives as well, although we don't always see it. God is putting together a package in each of our lives, preparing us to make a unique contribution to his kingdom. We need to ask ourselves, *What have I come to the kingdom for? Why has God brought me to this particular time and place?*

Approaching life situations in this way represents a radical shift in thinking for some of us. We are more accustomed to thinking, *But I'm so limited. God could never use me!* Many factors cause us to feel limited or inadequate: a lack of formal education, a late start in the Christian life, our marital status, financial limitations, young children or rebellious teens in the home, a lack of self-confidence and so on. But these are only perceived limitations. Often what we see as limitations are God's training ground for unique usefulness to him.

Joni Eareckson Tada has discovered that her limitations are inextricably interwoven with God's purposes for her life. As a young girl of seventeen, she was paralyzed from the neck down in a diving accident. Facing the rest of her life as a quadriplegic confined to a wheelchair, she raged against God and wished to take her own life. But as she allowed God to deal with her at her point of deepest pain, she found that the limitations of her disabled body propelled her into ministry to others who were disabled. She found that they listened to her in a way that they wouldn't listen to someone whose body was whole. Now she has an international ministry to a group of people who up to this point had been largely unreached for Christ. God brought her to a time and a place in a disabled body for a purpose.

No matter what our circumstances, then, we still need to ask ourselves, *What have I come to the kingdom for?* Generally speaking, we have all come to this time and place as servants of Jesus Christ, as investors of what he has given us. But we need to go beyond the general, get down to specifics and ask ourselves: *What gifts, experiences, opportunities and burdens is God blending together in my life to make me of special use to him?* As we begin to live into the answers to this question, we are beginning to discover our calling, our vocation.

IDENTIFYING GOD'S PURPOSES

Parker Palmer talks about "hearing the voice of vocation" when he describes the dynamic of discovering God's purposes for our lives. "Discovering vocation does not mean scrambling toward some prize just beyond my reach but accepting the treasure of true self I already possess. Vocation does not come from a voice 'out there' calling me to become something I am not. It comes from a voice 'in here' calling me to be the person I was born to be, to fulfill the original selfhood given me at birth by God." We then have the opportunity to make choices to arrange our lives in ways that are consistent with the person God has created us to be and the good purposes that he has for us.

Paul describes this opportunity by saying: "Live life, then, with a due sense of responsibility, not as [those] who do not know the meaning of life but as those who do. Make the best use of your time, despite all the evils of these days. Don't be vague but grasp firmly what you know to be the will of the Lord" (Ephesians 5:15-17 Phillips). Let's look at four areas that will help us do that.

Purpose. A life purpose answers our larger questions about the meaning of life and the reasons for our existence. It reflects the overall vision God has given us for what he wants to do in and through our lives. Formulating a life purpose statement can't be rushed, because it is forged as we search the Scriptures and hear the Lord speak to us in a very personal way. It reflects the essence and uniqueness of who we are as created beings. Our deepest life purpose or calling will probably stay basically the same throughout the span of our life, although we may spend much time clarifying and deepening our understanding of that purpose so that we can live into it with greater joy and freedom.

Priorities. Since a life purpose statement is, by nature, rather general, it is also important to identify the specific priority areas through which these purposes will be accomplished: spiritual life, personal growth, family life, work, service in the church and the world. Then within these priority areas we can develop more specific purpose statements. If one of my larger purposes in life is to know God, I need to be more specific about what I am aiming for in this area. Do I need to learn to be quiet and just be in his presence? Do I want to develop a deeper prayer life? What character issues do I need to work on? In regard to my family, what exactly do I want my husband and children to receive from me and from our home life? As far as my contribution to my church and community is concerned, what gifts has God given me that need to be developed? How do those fit with the things I'm burdened about? And what about friendships, intellectual challenges and healthy living?

This is the place to dream the dreams that God is whispering to our hearts—even the ones that seem so far-fetched we're almost afraid to put them into words.

Planning. The process of identifying purposes and priorities doesn't guarantee that in reality we will spend our time and energy on those priorities. It is very easy to say, "I want to be more sexually responsive to my husband" or "I want to be a writer" or "I want to be more involved in my children's education." But it is quite another thing to take steps to make it so.

Goals help us plan our priorities into the minutes and hours of our days; they are the steps that will take us to the end result. An effective goal is reachable, measurable and realistic, taking into consideration our season of life and other factors that might affect our plans—health, transportation, finances, family priorities and so forth. If our goals are unrealistic, we set ourselves up for failure and discouragement.

For instance, one of the main purposes of my life is to serve God with my gifts. Since I understand that one of the ways I am to accomplish this is through writing, writing has become a priority. When the opportunity came along to write my first Bible study guide, I said yes because I could see how it fit into God's purposes for my life, but I needed a realistic plan that would take into account my busy season

of life. Since I had two young daughters, the only writing time I had
was in the early mornings before anyone was awake and in the afternoons while my older daughter was in preschool and my younger
daughter was napping. So my goal for accomplishing this writing
project was to write early in the morning five mornings a week and
during naptime three afternoons a week. It would be easy to tell if I
was accomplishing my goal from day to day. And I felt confident that
working at that pace, I would finish the project in a year.

Discipline. It was a great plan, but there was one problem. Quite
often when I took my older daughter to preschool, I would run into
a friend who was fun to be with and enjoyed shopping, as I do. If either one of us mentioned anything about shopping, we would throw
responsibility to the wind and go. As you can imagine, this greatly
hindered my work on the writing project (not to mention how hard
it was on our budget!). I had not yet come to grips with the fact that
saying yes to the goals and plans that would take me step by step toward God's purposes would also require saying no to things that in-
terfered. I finally realized that if I wanted the long-term satisfaction
of seeing my work in print, I would have to give up the short-term
pleasure of those spur-of-the-moment shopping trips. Every preschool day, I faced the choice between short-term pleasure and making the best use of my time. Sometimes I succumbed to temptation,
but I grew more consistent in sticking to my plan and eventually got
the job done.

Delaying self-gratification is one habit necessary to saying no,
but it's a difficult one to develop! And in saying no we sometimes
risk the disappointment of others. They may even think we are
wrong for not being available for the activities and projects they
think are important. Many women have been conditioned to be
"people pleasers" and, as such, find it very hard to hold on to their

own priorities in the face of pressure. But we must remember that others don't necessarily know the purposes to which God has called us or the commitments we are juggling. When we give in to pressure (whether from ourselves or from others), we are fitting into others' purposes rather than God's. Each one of us is responsible to God for what we do with the time and energy he has given us. People who are spiritually wise will trust him to move us to do what he is calling us to.

In *A Time for Risking,* Miriam Adeney comments, "Only those who turn down standard activities will have time and energy for priority affairs." She offers this challenge:

> For you, kingdom priorities might mean saying no to talking on the telephone so much. Or saying no to well-established committees in order to serve on more needy committees. Saying no to certain kinds of reading in order to do other, more crucial reading. Saying no to thinking so much about how you feel or about the way you look—saying no to your "pity parties." Kingdom priorities might mean monitoring your imagination and bringing every thought captive to Christ (2 Corinthians 10:5). It might mean limiting the time you spend thinking about fashion, shopping, romance, eating out, backpacking, gardening, skiing, soap operas, novels, gossip, or whatever catches your imagination, in order consciously to focus a certain amount of your thoughts on people's need for Jesus, on world hunger, on nuclear weapon dangers, on teenage mothers. Kingdom priorities may mean saying no to spending so much time with certain friends in order to spend time with friends who need you more. Or limiting your mindless conversations, in order consciously to make your conversations channels of grace.

This is not to say that there should be no time for fun and relaxation; we need some of that or we will burn out quickly. But in the context of purposeful living, relaxation is even more delicious because we give it to ourselves intentionally as one part of a life well lived. This too is part of our conscious choice to live in the balanced and fruitful way that God intended.

One way to become more intentional and disciplined about living your life according to God's purposes is to actually chart out your purposes, priorities and plans. Many tools on the market are designed to help with this process, but I have found that creating my own chart helps me solidify my thoughts and commitments. In addition to a written life purpose statement, I use a separate sheet of paper for each priority area (spiritual life, personal development, family, church, work, etc.) and then divide the paper into three columns. The first column contains my purpose statements (what I'm aiming for) in that area. The second contains my plan (specific goals and scheduling), and the third contains any disciplines involved (things I will need to say no to in order to say yes to what really matters).

SAYING YES TO GOD

Have you ever imagined what would have happened if some of the women in the Bible had said no to the purposes of God? What if Esther had said, "But Lord, I have myself set up pretty well here. I'm the queen and the king loves me. Why would I want to mess that up?" Or what if Deborah, when called to be a prophet, judge and military leader in Israel, had responded like this: "But Lord, don't you know that women aren't supposed to do those sorts of things?" And what about Mary, the mother of Jesus? "But God, this is extremely inconvenient: couldn't you wait until after I get married? This is going to ruin my reputation, and besides, I had a few things I wanted to do before I had kids!"

In any of these cases, history could have turned out quite differently. But these women did not allow themselves to be limited by the voices of cultural norms, personal convenience or fear. Rather, they embraced the package God had put together in their lives, and they responded when he called them to use it.

We may not be called to be Deborahs or Esthers, leading armies or thwarting great political schemes (although I wouldn't rule that out!). God may be putting our package together in such a way that we are uniquely prepared to confront injustice and immorality in our community, to mold a young life, to care unselfishly for aging parents, to serve Jesus by opening our home or to speak with discernment to the church. Knowing that God is in control of preparing us for his purposes adds value to many aspects of life that would otherwise be mundane. The young mother who is scraping Play-Doh off the floor can see it in the context of purpose—she has provided her child with an important tactile experience! A woman working in a job that isn't exactly a dream come true can take advantage of the character-building opportunities for spiritual growth. We can even clean the bathroom with an awareness that we are creating the atmosphere in our home that is important to us.

Of course, other opportunities will require more courage: speaking out publicly about something important, home schooling our kids if that's what's best for them, running for public office, sharing Christ with a neighbor or moving into the inner city in order to make a difference there.

Our challenge then is to say yes to the most important things, the things for which God has brought us to this time and place. In so doing, we make room in our life for meaning and value, and we will feel

God's pleasure upon us. Rather than the "torture of restlessness and vague desire," the wind of the Spirit will fill our sails and move us onto the high sea of purposeful living. Will it be frightening? At times, yes. Will it be risky? More so than staying in a quiet harbor. Will it be exhilarating? You bet! Will it be fulfilling? Well, let's put it this way: it's the only way to live.

SPIRITUAL EXERCISES

Alone with God

Silence. As you come to the end of this chapter, take a few moments to sit with God in the silence of your heart. Ask God to help you actually "see" the package he is putting together in your life. Think about what gifts, experiences, opportunities, burdens and passions make up the person you are. Allow enough time for this "package" to take on full detail and color in your mind and heart. Sit with whatever emotions come—joy, gratitude, awe and so on. You might experience some "negative" emotions such as sadness (that it's taken so long for you to see the package God is putting together in your life) or frustration (that you or others in your life can't quite see it yet). Don't censor yourself at all. Just "be with" the truth of your experience in the presence of God.

Read Psalm 139:13-18 and, to the extent that you are able, let the truth of this passage be true for you.

Prayer and journaling. Review the chapter that you have just read, noticing the places where you said, "I really want that!" (resonance) or "I'm not sure I'm ready for that" (resistance). In your journal, tell God about the thoughts, feelings, desires, hesitations and questions that this chapter raised for you.

- What does your reaction indicate about what is going on in the deeper places of your soul?

- In what way might God be saying, "I have brought you to the kingdom for just such a time as this"?

Invitations. God, how do you want me to hear you through this reading? Are you inviting me to respond to you in some way?

Serving God in the Way That He Calls

Dear God, Are boys better than girls? I know you are one, but please try
to be fair.

We still laugh about the time our oldest daughter, Charity, at two and a half, traipsed into church during a worship service wearing a diaper on her head. She was trailing behind as we slipped into our front-row seats a few minutes late, so we didn't realize that she was making this fashion statement until she had already caused a bit of a stir.

This was more than childhood silliness. Early in her young life she had observed that the women in our church (including her mother) wore head coverings, usually a veil of some sort. To her, putting something on her head was part of what it meant to be a woman.

I had grown up in a church setting that emphasized submission to men's authority as one of the central elements of mature womanhood. Being a woman meant wearing a head covering to symbolize this submission—and much more. It meant not being allowed to speak in church gatherings. It meant knowing that even though I was supposed to be a priest (according to 1 Peter 2:5, 9), men were the only ones allowed to perform the priestly functions of teaching, leading worship, serving Communion or offering an audible prayer when the church gathered. It meant hearing letters from women missionaries read in church services but finding that when they were home on furlough they could not get up in these same gatherings and give a report. It meant listening as the men were exhorted to step forward and accept their God-given responsibility of teaching and leading, and watching as the godly women I respected had to sit in numb silence.

All these rules, spoken and unspoken, sent a powerful message to a young, spiritually sensitive girl who was trying to figure out what it meant to be female and Christian. The message that I and the women around me internalized was not a very positive one.

A GROWING AWARENESS

A small Christian liberal arts college in the Midwest gave me the opportunity to experience, for the first time, an environment in which gender wasn't such a big issue. Women could speak and pray in chapel, serve as leaders in student government and receive equal encouragement from their professors. At the same time, my love for the church was growing, and I served there in any way I could. I realized that there was nothing I wanted more than to spend my life serving God among his people. So besides getting certified to teach, I took Bible, Greek and Christian education courses with a view to serving the church with greater effectiveness.

I emerged from college with great eagerness but soon discovered that while my male peers were groomed to serve as preachers, teachers and elders in my home church, women were relegated to a much narrower sphere of ministry. When young men demonstrated desire or ability to teach and lead the congregation, it was cause for celebration; when a young woman expressed these same desires, she was viewed as rebellious. I began to wonder if God had made a mistake in entrusting a woman with my particular gifts and desires for ministry.

It was even more disturbing to see that women did not have much voice in church life at all. It was painful when the men would retreat to another room to discuss important spiritual matters, leaving the women to tend to the kitchen and the children. The belief that women (by nature of their femaleness) functioned best behind the scenes and men (by virtue of their maleness) were best suited for up-front leadership didn't fit with my understanding of spiritual gifts and personality types. I couldn't help wondering, *Is the female perspective so devoid of value that Christian congregations can live without it?*

For many years I hid my struggle from other people's view, alternating between self-blame (was it my character flaws that kept me from being content with the traditional role carved out for women?) and anger at those who perpetrated such a discriminatory system. At the same time I kept serving in whatever capacity I was allowed: working with youth, teaching girls' Sunday school and women's Bible studies, directing vacation Bible school and women's ministries, playing piano, singing in the choir. While I enjoyed each of these ministry opportunities, I continued to experience a great deal of turmoil over women's lack of freedom to participate fully in all aspects of church life.

It was becoming a crisis of faith for me. After all, the church is *God's* church. Was this an accurate reflection of him? Was he really a chauvinistic father who allowed his sons to speak and participate in family decisions while barring his daughters from the same privileges? Was Eve's sin so much greater and more unforgivable than Adam's that the entire female gender must forever be treated with suspicion and controlling measures?

These were not the questions of a theologian; they were questions wrung from the heart of a daughter to her heavenly Father. I did not want to believe the conclusions to which some women of the time were arriving, yet their conclusions didn't surprise me. For example, one woman said, "I have read the Bible. The Christian slate is there for all to read and it cannot be wiped clean . . . for Christianity is a male religion, written by men, for men, with a male god."

As irreverent as it seemed to question God on these matters, that was never the attitude of my heart. These questions were getting in the way of the most important relationship in my life, and I needed to ask them. Fortunately, I knew God well enough to be confident that he was big enough and loving enough to help me find the answers.

A TIME TO STUDY

Finally, the time came for me to quit stewing and start studying. An invitation to develop Bible study materials for the women in my church gave me the opportunity to pore over the Scriptures from beginning to end, studying anything and everything that had to do with women. My heart was stirred by women in the Bible such as Abigail, Deborah, Huldah, Esther and Priscilla, who made an impact for God's kingdom as they acted in courageous ways that even now strike us as outside the normal "woman's role." I marveled at the freedom they found to follow the Lord's call. I found myself weeping with love for Jesus as I witnessed the respect with which he treated women. And through my study of spiritual gifts, I began to discover that *God gives gifts not based on gender but based on the work he has called us to do.*

What I was learning from studying the full breadth of Scripture just didn't fit with the emphasis on the silence and subordination of women with which I had grown up. After I finished writing that Bible study, I kept right on studying until I came to the point where I understood enough to be at peace with God, to follow his call on my own life with courage and to teach my daughters that they too could

become anything that God called them to be. As women, we all need
to know at least that much.

Creation. I began my study with creation, for it is there that we get
our first glimpses of what it means to be human beings created male
and female. In Genesis 1 and 2 we see God's original and best plan
for gender relations: a partnership model in which a man and a
woman function as a team of equals. In Genesis 1, we learn that God
created humankind in two sexes—male and female—and that both
were created equally in his image (verses 26-27). God blessed the
man and the woman and gave them both the responsibility to be
fruitful and multiply, to fill the earth, subdue it and rule together over
all living things (verses 28-29). When God surveyed all that he had
made, including his newest addition of this marriage team, for the
first time in the entire creation process he commented that it was
"very good" (verse 31).

Genesis 2 gives a more detailed account of the creation of man and
woman. Verse 18 tells us God recognized that it was not good for
man to be alone, and so he created woman—"a helper suitable for
him" (NIV). While some theologians have interpreted this passage to
mean that woman was somehow subordinate to man because she was
created to be his helper *(ezer),* elsewhere in Scripture the same Hebrew word *(ezer)* is most often used in reference to God himself. For
example, in Exodus 18:4, Jethro names his son Eliezer because "the
God of my father was my help *[ezer].*" And in Psalm 40:17, as in
many other places, the psalmist refers to God as "my help *[ezer]* and
my deliverer." The word *ezer* is translated in other places in Scripture
as "succorer," "rescuer," "deliverer," "strength" and "power."

In contemporary usage the word *helper* often connotes strength. A
parent helps a child with his homework. A doctor helps a patient get
well. A rich nation helps refugees who come to their country. A per-

son who is in distress psychologically or spiritually looks to a pastor or a counselor for help. "The one who helps is the one who has something to *offer* the one who is helpless or needs help. Adam needed help. He had no partner. God created a partner—a helper. There is no hint of either superiority or subordination."

When God brought Eve to Adam, he was astounded and overjoyed to find someone who was like him: "This is now bone of my bones, / And flesh of my flesh" (Genesis 2:23 NASB). But he also recognized and named the gender difference when he called her "Woman, because she was taken out of Man." It was because of their fundamental unity that men were henceforth instructed to leave their own family and cleave or cling to their wife (verse 24). Rather than pull a woman into the authority structure of his family (the norm in the patriarchal system that developed later), the man is the one who moves away from his family toward his wife, according to Genesis, and clings to her in a new relationship characterized by interdependence. "Therefore a man leaves his father and his mother and clings to his wife, and they become one flesh" (2:24).

Paul expands on this interdependence in 1 Corinthians 11:11-12 when he points out that "in the Lord, neither is woman independent of man, nor is man independent of woman. For as the woman originates from the man, so also the man has his birth through the woman" (NASB). This interdependence is pictured in the phrase "and they shall become one flesh." Nothing here suggests that one is "over" the other. In fact, any introduction of hierarchy seems completely contradictory to the oneness and interdependence pictured here.

The Fall. Eve's choice and Adam's choice to disobey God caused dire consequences for the human race. Among these was the introduction of sin and guilt, shame and blame into the male-female relationship. Although popular interpretations of this incident have taught that Eve was somehow "more guilty" than Adam because she ate the fruit first and then offered it to him, Genesis 3:6 reveals that Adam was with Eve during her temptation, apparently offering no help. Eve was left to hold her own in conversation with the serpent, and when she offered Adam the fruit, he took it without argument: "she also gave some to her husband, who was with her, and he ate."

When Paul observed that "it was not Adam who was deceived, but the woman being deceived, fell into transgression" (1 Timothy 2:14 NASB), the question comes to mind, which is worse: to sin knowingly or to be deceived? If Paul is attributing "greater guilt" to Eve, how are we to interpret Romans 5:12-19 ("sin came into the world through one man") and other passages in which Paul ascribes primary guilt to Adam? This apparent contradiction can be resolved by recognizing that Adam and Eve were equally responsible for their personal choices in the Garden of Eden.

The consequences of the Fall outlined in Genesis 3:14-19 are *predictions* of how things would be in a sinful world rather than a prescription or a commandment for how God wanted things to be. In no way does this description of these natural consequences mean that women are prohibited from seeking ways to avoid the pain of childbirth or freeing themselves from wrongful domination by their husband. By the same token, God predicted that men would have to work very hard to get the ground to bear fruit, but he did not prohibit them from seeking ways to make work easier—which they have. More significant, within this sad scenario came another prediction— a promise even!—that one day Someone would come who would break the power of the evil one (Genesis 3:15). That Someone has come, and the church is still discovering how his life, death and resurrection can redeem all areas of life—including relationships between the sexes.

The life of Christ. In Old Testament days, the effects of sin in the lives of men and women were clearly seen. Women were viewed and treated as possessions—as "less than" men. Consequently, they were victims of terrible abuse and violence (Genesis 16; 19:1-8; Judges 11:29-40; Judges 19). Even so, women like Miriam, Huldah, Abigail, Esther and Deborah demonstrated that "you can't keep a good woman down." When a woman was the right person for the job, whether it was leading in worship, prophesying, exhorting, saving a nation from genocide or leading soldiers into battle, God didn't hesitate to use her. And the results were impressive.

This reality was all but lost on Jewish men who, at the time of Christ, were still thanking God regularly "that I was not born a woman." They were forbidden to teach the words of the law to a woman publicly.

When Christ came, he broke man-made rules for gender relations and made new ones that more accurately reflected God's heart toward women. That is why we see Jesus talking to an immoral woman about theology, worship, the state of her relationships and the state of her soul (John 4). That is why we see him pointing out to men that a woman caught in adultery was no more guilty than they were (John 8:1-11), and why we see him receiving Mary's act of worship as much more meaningful than anything that was going on in the synagogues (John 12:1-8). That is why some of his best friends were women— women were last at the cross and first at the tomb (Mark 15:40-47). And he appeared first to a woman and gave her the joyful responsibility of informing the disciples that he was alive (Mark 16:1-8)!

Christ, who was God come to earth in human form, was untainted by the sexism that characterized the society in which he lived. He raised a new standard for men and women to follow in their relationships. The impact of his life on gender relations can be summed up in Galatians 3:27-28: "For all of you who were baptized into Christ have clothed yourself with Christ. There is neither Jew nor Greek, there is neither slave nor free man, there is neither male nor female; for you are all one in Christ Jesus" (NASB). These words are revolutionary from a cultural, political and religious standpoint. The church is still in the process of applying these verses as we deal with the discrimination and partiality (all kinds) that exist in direct contradiction to the equality spoken of here.

The new community. After Christ's death, the disciples returned to Jerusalem to await the Holy Spirit. Acts 1:14 says that they "all with one mind were continually devoting themselves to prayer, along with the women" (NASB). When the day of Pentecost came, they were all together in one place, and tongues of fire rested on each one of them. All of them were filled with the Holy Spirit and were speaking in tongues (Acts 2:4). When Peter got up to preach, he explained these events to those who were watching. He said that this was a fulfillment of Joel's prophecy that when God poured forth his Spirit on all humanity, sons and daughters, men and women would prophesy—that is, speak forth the mind of God (Acts 2:16-18). And they did!

As the early church grew, women worked right alongside the men in spreading the gospel and planting churches. In many cases it was a woman (such as Lydia in Philippi) who was the prime mover in getting a church started and hosting it in her home. Other women taught theology (Priscilla), served as ministers or deacons (Phoebe), prophesied (Philip's daughters) and simply worked very hard (see Romans 16:1-16).

First Corinthians 12 puts into words what was already in evidence in the early church: to each one is given the manifestation of the Spirit (spiritual gift) without regard to gender. It was entirely consistent with Peter's assertion that "God is not one to show partiality"

(Acts 10:34 NASB) and that we are all members of the royal priesthood, called out of darkness by God to proclaim his excellencies (1 Peter 2:9-10).

When Paul described the body of Christ in 1 Corinthians 12 and Ephesians 4, it was much more than just a theory—it was the way the men and women in the early church had worked together from the very beginning. Like the early church, we too can embrace a community that celebrates and uses the gifts of everyone. The fact that men and women can work together is one of the truths that can set us free.

Redemption. At the heart of the gospel is a message of freedom for all who are oppressed (Galatians 5:1), and one doesn't need to look far to see that women have been greatly oppressed. Not only did Christ model a new kind of relationship between men and women, but through his death he also redeemed us from the oppressive effects of the curse (Galatians 3:13). *When we require women to pay over and over again for Eve's transgression with their silence and submission, we negate the full redemptive power of the gospel.* Rather than becoming an example of relationships that have been redeemed, we model the curse. Rather than living out God's ideal (as seen in Genesis 1) so that our presence in society begins to transform it, we allow ourselves to be squeezed into the world's mold of sexism and discrimination.

Several biblical texts can be confusing as we seek to understand how men and women are to function together in marriage, ministry and society. One of the most difficult to interpret is 1 Timothy 2:11-12, which seems to say that women are not allowed to teach or exercise authority over men. While study of this particular passage and others is extremely important, basic principles of biblical interpretation teach us that we must always interpret difficult passages in light of broad theological themes such as the ones we have just observed—

themes rooted in creation, the character of God (his justice and im-
partiality), the life and teachings of Christ, the leading of the Holy
Spirit in the early church, and general New Testament teaching regarding spiritual gifts and the priesthood of all believers.

An examination of Scripture's themes reveals that "more than a
hundred passages in the Bible affirm women in roles of leadership,
and fewer than half a dozen appear to be in opposition." Yet as Christians, we have built an elaborate system of belief and practice on only
a few passages, such as 1 Timothy 2:11-12 and 1 Corinthians 11:2-
16. These passages have loomed so large that we have allowed them
to color everything else we read. I am not suggesting we merely dismiss these passages because we do not understand them. They are
still part of the Scriptures, and we must continue to wrestle with their
true meaning. (For a fuller discussion of 1 Timothy 2:11-12, see appendix A.) But an even greater temptation is the temptation to lift
these passages out of their own context, out of the context of the
broader themes of Scripture, or to elevate them to the point that they
become more important than the overall message of the Scriptures.

Understanding the subjective elements of the translation process
should, at the very least, make us cautious about developing an elaborate system of rules for gender relations based on words that have a
range of possible meanings and passages that seem to be at odds with
other Scriptures. Indeed, it should lead to a desire to explore any new
evidence—such as the continuing discoveries made by linguists and
translators—and trusting the Holy Spirit to lead us into truth.

Since we understand from other Scriptures (such as 1 Corinthians
11:5) that women did pray and prophesy in church, Paul would have
been contradicting himself if he were saying that women could not
teach or be in positions of authority both now and forever. Additional
information about historical context, meanings of keywords and

grammatical structure (such as the material in appendix A) helps us understand that Paul was addressing the *content* of their teaching, since he was speaking to the issue of heresy that was swirling around this fledgling church. He was also addressing the manner in which any new believers should learn—quietly and in submission to the authority of Scripture.

This in itself was the start of something new. Ordinarily Jewish women were not taught the Scriptures. But now Paul is saying that women who were new to the faith should be encouraged to learn quietly until they were ready to participate fully in the life of the church, as mature women such as Phoebe (Romans 16:1-2) and Priscilla (Acts 18:24-26) were already doing.

COMING OUT ON THE OTHER SIDE

The process of searching for truth is never as linear as it sounds. My theological and intellectual journey had an emotional and spiritual side as well. Perhaps the fact that I was a preacher's kid and experienced my church almost as extended family made it more difficult for me than for some women to ask the questions I needed to ask, to claim my beliefs and then live them out. Even as things became clearer theologically, I was aware that I had a lot to lose.

I had to face the fact that I might lose the respect of those who would categorize me as "a liberal" or "a feminist"—whatever such ill-defined categories might mean. Opportunities for ministry might be fewer, at least in the short term, as people responded and reacted to the fact that I was taking a position on this controversial subject.

I knew that some of my significant relationships would be affected as well. It would require hard work to process the changes that were taking place in my life in response to the truth that I was trying to live into. I already knew that some might not have the flexibility to accommodate the freedom I was finding as I responded to God's call beyond what was traditionally viewed as acceptable for women. All of a sudden I began to understand more clearly what Jesus meant when he taught his disciples about the radical nature of following him— sometimes it means the willingness to *leave* those we love in order to follow God's risky invitations. I had always assumed that this teaching had to do with *physically* leaving to follow God's call to a foreign mission field or an opportunity for service across the country. But now I had to grapple with the fact that sometimes following God's risky invitations has to do with challenging ideology or theology that is too small to contain God's truth, breaking with tradition that limits God's expression of the life he wants to live through us, or disappointing the expectations of those who thought they understood God's will for us.

The awareness of what I had to lose caused me to hesitate, and the place in which I hesitated was full of the anger and fragmentation that comes when we do not live out of our core beliefs. I couldn't pray. I couldn't worship. All I could do was shout my questions and wrestle with the Scriptures and God himself.

And there was grief. Grief over a world that should have been and could have been, but wasn't—a world where a young woman could pour out her love for God in service with no thought to gender. Grief over the time I had spent stewing over these things rather than serving. And eventually even a grief and need to repent for the mistakes I had made along with a need to forgive the mistakes of others as we all went through this process of growth.

Then one spring afternoon, several years after I had begun my search in earnest, the Holy Spirit communicated with me in the deep places of my soul, that place where God's Spirit witnesses with our spirit with sighs or utterances that are beyond words. It was a way of communicating that I had grown to recognize and trust throughout these years of quiet listening, an unmistakable impression upon my spirit: "I have spent years teaching you and leading you into truth. Now let that truth lead you out of this valley. It is time to stand for what you believe and never look back." If it had been any clearer, it would have been audible.

So I left the valley of darkness and unfreedom to stand on the truth that the Holy Spirit had spoken to my heart: the truth that *women and men are equally sinful and yet equally redeemed for full participation in every facet of life, love and service.* As painful as the process had been, how glad I was that I had taken the time to wrestle with God over these issues. For like Jacob, who had wrestled with God's angel or God himself (Genesis 32:24), I walked away with the blessing of knowing where I stand in the presence of God and in the community

---

FOR WOMEN WHO WANT TO KNOW GOD MORE DEEPLY AND TO PARTICIPATE IN SHAPING THE NEXT GENERA- TION OF WOMEN FOR CHRIST, THERE IS NOTHING MORE IMPORTANT THAN KNOWING HOW GOD VIEWS US AND WHETHER WE ARE FREE TO SERVE HIM IN THE WAY THAT HE CALLS US.

---

of faith. Like Jacob, I have a painful place that is still sensitive, re- minding me of the wrestling I have done. But I wouldn't trade this part of my journey for anything, because understanding this truth has become a necessary part of growing in my love for God and in the freedom of serving him wholeheartedly. It's hard to worship a God whom you do not feel free to serve.

A FOUNDATIONAL TRUTH

For women who want to know God more deeply and to participate in shaping the next generation of women for Christ, there is nothing more important (aside from the issue of salvation) than knowing how God views us and whether we are free to serve him in the way that he calls us. The way we answer this question affects all areas of life: self-esteem, emotions, our relationships with husband, children and parents, worship and service to God, and our view of ourselves at work and in society. It just doesn't get any more foundational than that!

There will come a day when women will enjoy the full rights of God that "sons" know—those who receive the blessing of their family inheritance. And in that day, it will be hard to remember a time when anyone was barred from ministry or other life callings simply because they were women. Jesus said, "You will know the truth, and the truth will set you free" (John 8:32 NIV). History shows us that freedom never comes without a fight. But it does come.

SPIRITUAL EXERCISES

Alone with God

Silence. As you come to the end of this chapter, take a few moments to sit with God in the silence of your heart and reflect on one or more of these questions:

- What are some of your earliest memories of yourself as a little girl growing up, noticing and learning about what it meant to be a woman?

- Where did the strongest messages come from?

- What emotions do you feel as you scroll back through your childhood and notice these things?

- What was your experience in the midst of these messages and experiences?
- Did you identify God with any aspect of these messages, or did you find him to be different from what you were experiencing?

Prayer and journaling. Review this chapter, noticing the places of resonance and resistance that you highlighted. In your journal, tell God about the thoughts, feelings, desires and questions that this chapter has raised for you. Notice the places where your experiences and questions were the same as or different from the author's. Allow yourself to experience any emotions that come and to explore without judgment the source(s) of your emotions with words or by drawing pictures.

- What might your reaction indicate about what is going on in the deeper places of your soul?
- What is God inviting you to look at in yourself and in your experiences as a woman?

Invitations. God, are you inviting me to hear or do anything in response to what I have read in this chapter?

Living in Truth

In a restaurant let your mate or date do the ordering. You may know more about vintage wine than the wine steward, but if you are smart you'll let your man do the choosing and be ecstatic over his selection, even if it tastes like shampoo.

ARLENE DAHL, *ALWAYS ASK A MAN*

Do not lie to one another, seeing that you have stripped off the old self with its practices and have clothed yourselves with the new self, which is being renewed in knowledge according to the image of its creator.

COLOSSIANS 3:9-10

One of my earliest moments of awareness that women have distinct challenges relative to telling the truth came when I was in my late twenties. My husband and I had been identified as potential leaders in our fledgling church, so we were invited to take a class on leadership taught by the pastor. As a part of this class we were invited to take the Performax (DISC) personality test in order to understand our leadership style better. We learned that according to this test, there are four personality types: D (dominant, Type A personality), I (influencing), S (steady) and C (compliant). Each of us has one of these as our primary personality type and another that is secondary.

The results of my test were unmistakable: I definitely had the high D (dominant), Type A personality. This wasn't exactly news to me; I was aware that my gifts and personality traits clustered around leadership. However, I had spent years trying to tone down that part of my personality. After all, what Christian woman wants to be called dominant when compliance and submissiveness are so much more highly valued in women? It took me a week to get over my embarrassment once everyone knew my well-kept secret. My only comfort was the knowledge that most people in the class had guessed that I was an I personality (influencing, inspirational), which seemed to be a lot more acceptable in a woman. I congratulated myself on the fact that I had done a pretty good job of hiding myself.

I HAD TO FACE THE FACT THAT I HAD AN UNEASY
RELATIONSHIP WITH TRUTH.

This moment was startling in its clarity, because I had to face the fact that I had an uneasy relationship with truth. In fact, I had to acknowledge that it was more natural for me to try to make reality palatable to others based on their sensitivities than to live fully and freely in the truth—whatever it was in any given moment. As I began to pay attention to how I lived in ways that were less than truthful, I noticed that I wasn't the only one.

Linda, a beautiful woman in her forties, used similar tactics for trying to manage the truth of who she was within her marriage. "My husband has always been a quiet man, and I've always been outgoing and involved. I enjoy being in the center of things, but I've learned to be quiet so that he can be the leader and my children can see that he is the head of our home."

I could hear the wistfulness in her voice as she talked about her accomplishments involving leadership and communication during her high school and young adult years. She wanted me to understand that those strengths were just as much a part of her as was this newly chosen "quietness." Although she intended for her comments and behavior to be respectful of her husband, they really communicated the opposite. I couldn't help thinking, *You mean the only way your husband can be a leader is for you to withhold your strength?* It just didn't seem honest. Did her husband know of this sadness that surfaced every now and then when she remembered lost opportunities for personal development? He was a loving husband; how would he feel if he ever realized that the price of his development was his wife's atrophy?

As distressing as Linda's comments were, I could relate to her need to minimize her strengths. I became more and more curious about the dynamics that cause many women—including myself—to hide the truth or at least soften or minimize it. I was reminded of a Bible story that provides a window of insight into the dynamics and also the results of the struggle with truth-telling that women seem to share across the generations.

You may be familiar with the story of Rebekah, who was married to Isaac. Together they had twin sons, Esau and Jacob. The problem was that they each had a favorite. Isaac preferred Esau because he was a hunter, and Rebekah favored Jacob, perhaps because he stayed closer to home. This favoritism brought out the worst in everyone—especially Rebekah. She was determined that her favorite, Jacob, would get the blessing that traditionally belonged to Esau as the first-born. God had already promised that Jacob would get the blessing

(Genesis 25:23), but rather than trusting and waiting for God to fulfill his purposes, Rebekah decided to help things along.

When Isaac was old, nearly blind and ready to bestow his blessing on Esau, Rebekah sent Jacob to his father masquerading as Esau, so that he would receive his brother's blessing. Jacob carried off the whole charade with precision. Shortly after Isaac had finished blessing Jacob, Esau returned from the fields ready to receive his blessing, and Isaac realized that there was something dreadfully wrong. He began to tremble violently as his mind pieced together what had happened and he realized that he had irreversibly blessed the wrong son (Genesis 27:33).

When Esau heard what had happened, "he cried out with an exceedingly great and bitter cry, and said to his father, 'Bless me, me also, father!' " (verse 34). Bur it was too late. Isaac had to give Esau the devastating news that his brother had come deceitfully and taken away his blessing. With gut-wrenching emotion Esau pleaded with his father to bless him with at least one blessing. Isaac did bless him, but it fell far short of the blessing Esau should have received (27:39-40), and it did nothing to heal the wounds that Rebekah and Jacob's manipulation had inflicted. Esau was so full of rage against Jacob that he purposed to kill him after Isaac's death. In order to protect Jacob, Rebekah sent him away, hoping that Esau's fury would eventually die down.

In a time and culture where women had little power, Rebekah may have felt that this was the only way she could have influence; however, her manipulation cost her dearly. She lost her opportunity to trust God and see him come through with his best. She forfeited her integrity. She failed to be an influence for good in the lives of those she loved. And she jeopardized every relationship that was important to her. As far as we know, when she sent Jacob away to escape Esau's murderous rage, it was the last time she saw her favored son. And in a turn of poetic justice, Jacob was deceived years later when his father-in-law-to-be gave him the wrong daughter as a bride (Genesis 29:15-30), which set off rivalry between sisters that embittered their home for decades.

GAMES WOMEN PLAY

Why is it that women often feel they have to resort to subtlety, indirectness or even deceit to get what they want? One reason is that we receive strong messages from our culture encouraging us to pretend to be something we're not. As psychologist Harriet Goldhor Lerner analyzes it, there are certain aspects of women's socialization that quite naturally result in this kind of behavior: "Pretending reflects deep prohibitions, real and imagined, against a more direct and forthright assertion of self. . . . 'Pretending' is so closely associated with 'femininity' that it is, quite simply, what the culture teaches women to do."

Our schooling in the fine art of manipulation and pretending often began at home. We may have been discouraged from stating our wants and needs too clearly and directly—because it was "unladylike." Instead we learned to drop hints and find devious ways to get what we wanted.

When you add these cultural messages to the ones that many of us received as a part of our religious upbringing, it's no wonder that we are a little hesitant about full disclosure!

GOD'S ALTERNATIVE TO PLAYING GAMES

Authentic relationships—honest, safe, empathic—provide some of the greatest joy and fulfillment that we can experience in this life. Yet ironically, in our desire to cultivate such relationships, sometimes we opt for peace at any price because it seems less risky. Somehow it even seems more "Christian" to hide the truth about ourselves, to deny feelings and to overlook offenses in an effort to avoid rocking the boat. However, when we skirt the truth and play games, the depth that we long for in our relationships will never develop.

From the Scriptures we learn that the key to deep and meaningful relationships is truth-telling. It is only as we speak the truth in love that we grow up in relation to others, become knit together with them and can each offer our particular strengths to the process of working together (Ephesians 4:15). But unfortunately, playing with the truth comes more naturally to us than truth-telling. Why? Because telling the truth is scary, especially in relationships in which truth has not been the pattern. We may think along these lines:

- If I told my boss that I don't appreciate his suggestive comments, I could get passed over for a promotion.

- If I told my parents it still bothers me that they were too busy for me, they would get mad and deny it.

- If I told my friend that some of her comments hurt me, she would just think I am overly sensitive.

- If I admitted to my small group that I am really struggling, they wouldn't think I was very spiritual.

- If I told my husband that I would like to pursue some of my own interests, he would panic.

- If I admitted how disturbed I am over the fact that we don't have any women elders at church, everyone would think I'm a feminist.

Yes, truth-telling can be frightening, but the alternative is much worse. When we cannot bring ourselves to tell the truth, our relationships will stay at a surface level at best—or, even more likely, they will deteriorate and die. Misunderstandings arise but are never resolved. Feelings beg to be expressed but are left to fester inside. Offenses occur but nobody talks about them. Our true personality is hidden and never invited to flourish in the warmth of acceptance. Avoidance patterns set in. Hurt and misunderstanding lead to detachment, distrust and bitterness. And love begins to die.

A realistic look at the results of game playing motivates us to take courage in hand and cultivate greater levels of truth in our relationships.

TRUTH IN THE INWARD BEING

Truth-telling begins with telling *ourselves* the truth. Psalm 51:6 reminds us that God desires truth in the inward being—truth about our beliefs and doubts, truth about what is happening in our relationships, truth about how we feel, what bothers us and how we need to change. It also includes telling God the truth, for as we learn to speak truthfully with God, we begin being more honest with ourselves. The experience of talking to Someone who loves us unconditionally, coupled with the deep work of the Holy Spirit (whose job it is to lead us into truth), causes things to become clearer and leads us to greater honesty with ourselves.

It is fascinating to observe the healing powers of truth-telling in the life of David. In Psalm 73, for example, David is consumed by jealousy toward wicked people whose lives seem to be going very well while he, a man who is trying to live a godly life, seems to have one problem after another. He rages on and on for fourteen verses, laying it all out before God. Finally, in the quiet that usually follows a true catharsis, God showed him a bigger picture, a picture that included a long-range perspective ("Then I perceived their end . . . how they are destroyed in a moment," verses 17, 19), self-knowledge ("I was like a brute beast toward you," verse 22) and heightened spiritual awareness ("There is nothing on earth that I desire other than you. My flesh and my heart may fail, but God is the strength of my heart," verses 25-26). No wonder David concluded that "for me it is good to be near God" (verse 28), for it was in his most honest moments that God was able to teach him wisdom "in my inmost place" (Psalm 51:6 NIV). And so it is with us.

TELLING OUR TRUE STORIES

Sometimes the hardest truth to tell ourselves and others is the truth about our experiences as women. So much of our literature, history, political context and theology has been written and developed from a male perspective that we struggle to find a voice of our own—to talk about life the way we see it. Men have translated the Scriptures for us. Male pastors and teachers tell us how we should feel about being mothers. Male doctors evaluate our physical health and tell us how to be sexually fulfilled. Male psychologists develop theories that tell us what it means to be psychologically well. We accept the roles assigned to us and believe it when we are told there must be something wrong with us if we're not satisfied with them. But every so often we wonder: *Why doesn't this fit for me? Why is mothering such a struggle for me? Why do I feel "less than" in my family, my church or my work? Why am I uncomfortable going to a man for pastoral care? Why does fitting into the role carved out for me seem like shoving a square peg into a round hole? And why don't we hear the stories about all the brave, strong things women have done for God and humankind? Why are their struggles and triumphs saved for the women's coffee hour?*

When questions like these surface for ourselves or for others, it seems much safer to silence them with thoughts or words like *Don't be ridiculous. This is what's best for us—everybody says so!* But where is

"truth in the inward being" (Psalm 51:6) if we don't give ourselves
and others the freedom to ask our truest questions, to raise a hand
(however timidly) and say, "Maybe that works for you, but my experience, my story, is very different"?

It is hard to tell the truth when all the voices around us seem to be
saying something different. I know because I've tried it. As I have already related, one of the hardest truths I have ever struggled to tell
myself, God, my husband and others was how much it was hurting
me to be a woman in the evangelical Christian subculture in which I
had been raised. From my preteen years on I had been noticing that
there was something terribly wrong with the way women were
treated in the church, and it was tearing my soul apart. But the truth
I was trying to tell about myself and the questions I was trying to ask
were labeled "rebellion" almost as soon as I uttered them, so I would
quickly withdraw them and stuff them down for a while longer.

It took me years to come right out and say that I just didn't believe
all that I had been taught about "a woman's place" in marriage and in
the church, that I saw something different when I read the Scriptures.
But how does a woman go about exploring the truth of her experiences when everyone around her says she is wrong and "shouldn't
feel that way"? Or when other women insist that their lives are completely fulfilling and the whole system is working for them?

At the time, I believed that other women were as satisfied as they
said they were, but now I know that they also struggled. Some kept
a stiff upper lip in public and cried their bitter tears alone. Some tried
to tell their stories to the powers that be but found that they were
never really heard. Others melted away quietly from Christian fellow-
ships, not always sure of the forces at work against them but knowing
they would die inside if they stayed. The few brave souls who refused
to be silenced had been so completely excised that I was aware of

them only to the extent that they had been labeled liberal and dangerous. Understandably, I felt very much alone in my turmoil—as though I were the strange one.

It wasn't until I was grown and well established in ministry that women began to tell me their true stories. A fiftyish woman who had taught with passion "Wives, submit to your husbands in all things" cried on my couch about a husband who made major life decisions without even consulting her. A mature single woman told me about having ministry opportunities withheld because she didn't have a man to team with. Several gifted women communicators told me about their rage and tears over being silenced in the church but asked me not to quote them because they feared the consequences of such honesty. A middle-aged woman admitted that her whole identity had been wrapped up in her children, and now that they were gone she was struggling desperately to keep depression at bay. As the director of women's ministry at one church where I served, I was cornered by a new Christian after a church service and was asked in hushed tones, "Could you tell me why we don't have any women pastors or elders? I mean, I love our pastors, but I could never go to one of them if I needed to talk about a problem." A young married woman told me of the husband who hit her when he got mad and the pastoral counselor who asked, "Well, what are you doing that causes him to do that?" And well into my married life, my own mother began to realize that wifely submission—as it had been taught in her generation—was an inadequate foundation for healthy relationships.

Why hadn't I heard these true stories when I needed them most—when I needed to know that my questions were legitimate and my unfolding story wasn't so unusual after all? Who was benefiting from this conspiracy of silence? And where is wholeness and integrity when we as women say we believe something and uphold it on an intellectual level but on an experiential level know it doesn't work?

It is very difficult to challenge what has already been accepted in society as the whole truth. Carol Gilligan, in her book *In a Different Voice,* demonstrates the impact of this problem in the field of psychology. She notes that psychological theory has been developed largely from the study of men, so that women never seem to fit existing models of human growth. Rather than recognizing the imbalance in the studies, experts had assumed that the problem was with women's development.

Lerner puts it this way: "Once something is defined as unfeminine or gender inappropriate, the old rules cannot easily be challenged. When women differ from the theories, the exceptions only prove rather than probe the rule, and it is the women—not the theories—who are brought into question. Women are still trying to fit into the predominant theories of the day rather than the other way around." This at least partially explains why it can be frightening to present a different view from what is normally accepted; there is always the very distinct possibility that someone will say, "The problem is not with the way things are; the problem is you."

TRUTH, INTEGRITY AND WHOLENESS CALL TO US JUST
LIKE FRESH AIR CALLS TO US ON A SPRING DAY.

In addition, "females in our culture are reinforced in their avoidance of their own power. Not openly expressing dissent (or a different view of reality) is applauded as being cooperative, and not risking hurting others is seen as being self-sacrificial. . . . For men, being seen as outspoken is not felt as pejoratively as it is for women."

There are very real reasons that we find it so hard to speak the truth about our experiences and questions. Yet truth, integrity and wholeness call to us just like fresh air calls to us on a spring day. Integrity or wholeness is a strong theme in the Bible. Proverbs 20:7 states, "The righteous walk in integrity." William Backus points out that *integrity,* as it is used in such verses, means "manifesting in life and words the truth." He continues: "The word *integrity* comes from the Latin *integer* meaning a whole number, not a fraction. The concept behind integrity is wholeness. When a person is the same without and within, when what others know about [her] is the same as what [she] knows about [herself], [she] has integrity." When we lack a true understanding of ourselves and are afraid to show others who we really are, we end up "faking it" much of the time, which leads to manipulation.

When we do work up the courage to be honest with ourselves and with others, our honesty may lead to a crisis of faith or, as Bill Hybels calls it, "the tunnel of chaos" in our relationship with God, with others and within ourselves. It certainly did for me. At times my own truth-telling took the form of angry shouting, lots of crying, unbelievable sadness, frenzied studying (because I just had to know) and admitting (much more than I wanted to) that I just *didn't* know. It tested my relationships to their limit. But God was deeper than the abyss I thought I was falling into, faith was stronger than my fears, and I did come out on the other side. When I first went into the tunnel of chaos ("where hurts are unburied, hostilities revealed, and tough questions asked"), I wasn't sure there would be anything on the other side.

But I found that even though it sometimes feels like I have more questions than answers, the air is clearer on the other side of the tunnel (life is pretty hazy when we're not telling the truth), and the world is bigger, so big that at times I can't get my arms around it. Truth is, after all, bigger than any of us. And I am more alive—spiritually, intellectually, emotionally, relationally—than I have ever been. That's what telling the truth does to you in the inward being.

TELLING EACH OTHER THE TRUTH

Telling ourselves and each other the truth—about who we are, how we feel, what we know, what we're questioning, what is working and what is tearing us apart in relationships and life—well, it takes raw courage at times. And it takes courage plus diligence and discipline to bring that kind of honesty into our everyday communications. Psychologist Backus points out that "our customs of speech frequently skirt the truth! We say, 'I'd love to have you come,' when we don't want the other person to come at all."

A good place to begin the journey toward greater truth in our relationships is to police ourselves for accuracy in our everyday communications. We can learn to let go of manipulative and less-than-honest communication patterns in favor of a more honest, straightforward approach. For instance:

- Instead of indirect communication such as dropping hints and "shoulding" ("You should stop watching so much television"), we can choose a more direct approach ("I am really concerned about how much time the television is on in our home. It seems to keep us from spending time talking, reading or doing other things together. Would you be willing to discuss setting some limits on the television?").

- Instead of "guilting" ("After all I do for you, the least you could do is . . ."), we can be honest about our feelings of being unappreciated ("Sometimes I feel like I do so much for you, but then when I need help, you're too busy. You probably don't mean it that way, but that's the way I'm feeling right now").

- Instead of withholding ourselves by administering the silent treatment, pouting or making ourselves sexually unavailable, we can talk about what is going on in the relationship ("I don't like it when you criticize me in public as you did today. It makes it very difficult for me to open up to you").

- Instead of intimidating, exaggerating or issuing ultimatums ("If you do that again, I'm quitting!"), we can say something that is more honest and realistic ("I am not willing to be verbally abused just to keep my job. If you do not stop, I will need to speak to our supervisor").

- Instead of secretly enlisting the help of others in pushing our agenda ("I just can't get through to my husband on this. Do you think you could talk to him about . . . ?"), we can talk directly to the person involved ("Since we seem to be stuck on this issue, would you be willing for the two of us to get help from a counselor?").

- Instead of telling those little white lies ("Sure, it will be no problem to take care of your kids this afternoon," when you know it could just put you over the edge), we can tell the truth ("I wish I could help you out, but I don't think I'd better take that on this afternoon").

- Instead of faking sexual enjoyment, we can be honest ("I'm really committed to having a great sex life with you, and that's why I need to tell you that this just isn't working for me. Could we try something else?").

At first these new communication patterns may feel as uncomfortable as a new pair of shoes, but the more we walk in them, the more comfortable they will become. Intimacy, trust and kinship will grow

because when we feel hurt, rather than withdrawing and losing closeness, we will talk about it, gain insight and establish new patterns
that protect love. When we say, "Yes, I would love to!" others won't
have to ask "Are you sure?" because they will know they can trust
what we say. And when, in the process of speaking truthfully, we get
glimpses of the true selves that are often hiding behind façades, we
will experience connection with fellow human beings that is un-
speakably fulfilling.

WHEN THE TRUTH IS HARD TO HEAR

Of course, the other side of our being "direct and forthright" is that
we welcome others to be just as honest with us. We need to demonstrate that authenticity and growth in our relationships are more important than the personal comfort that can be maintained only
through denial and defensiveness. We need to accept honest refusals
when they are given. And we need to listen and receive others in the
manner in which we want to be listened to and received.

I learned this lesson the hard way one Sunday when I deeply of-
fended some of the women in my church with comments I made during our weekend service. Speaking on the topic of "heroes," I made
the point that heroes are often people we look up to because they have
succeeded in areas in which we would like to succeed. To illustrate my
point, I mentioned a Christian author whose teaching on womanhood
and marriage I had respected until she had gotten a divorce. I mentioned that I no longer looked up to her in the way that I used to.

One woman who had gone through a divorce was so angry that
she couldn't wait until the service was over to speak with me. She left
her seat to request in whispered tones that we step into the hallway
to talk. Then, her voice trembling with emotion, she said, "Do you
have any idea what it was like to sit there with my children and listen

to what you said today? I have worked so hard to regain my dignity after my divorce, to create a stable life for my children and to find my place here in this church. Then to have you get up there and say that you didn't think you had anything to learn from someone like me! I had hoped that you could respect me and maybe learn something from my mistakes. And those of us who have gone through a divorce—well, we would like to be married again someday, and we would like to be able to learn from those of you who are still married about how to make a marriage work."

There was more, but I think you get the idea. It was a painful experience, but—praise God!—the first thing that happened (after I told myself to calm down and just listen) was that I saw myself in this dear woman.

I saw that her pain (of being viewed as "less than" in the church) was very similar to the pain I had experienced in the church all these years. The fact that I had been honest about my own pain made me much more sensitive to hers. I, too, had been an outsider—a woman in a male-dominated system. Here she was, another outsider (a divorced woman in a system that valued women who had managed to stay married) trying to tell her story to one of those insiders (a married woman who happened to be in charge of the women's ministry). It was a story I needed to hear.

Of course I would have liked to defend myself, as anyone would, but there was no adequate defense. My comments had been thoughtless and insensitive; the fact that I hadn't meant them to be was completely beside the point. I needed to listen to her pain, to hear myself through her ears as she sat in the auditorium that day and to tell her how sorry I was. I needed to tell her that yes, there was a lot I could learn from her and the struggles she had been through. In fact, I was already learning.

I shed tears that day. Some were tears of disappointment in myself for making such a hurtful mistake, some were tears for the women who came to church that day hoping for a word that would minister grace to their soul but instead received a barb. But there were also tears of gratefulness that this friend (and friend she was) didn't let me walk out the door ignorant of the pain I had caused, doomed to inflict it again at some other time and place.

I was honored that rather than letting our relationship go the way of churning anger that would eventually cool into numb distance, she struggled with the truth of her experience and then offered it to me. In that moment, I knew that even though the externals of our lives were so different, we were sisters who had many similarities. I knew that here was a friendship full of integrity—that when the truth needed to be told, this relationship could handle it. And I knew that the experience of hearing and being heard—of having an effect and being affected—was very rich for both of us that day, richer than any word I could have spoken from any podium.

A RICHER LIFE EXPERIENCE

The struggle toward truth-telling is at the center of our deepest longing for intimacy with others. It is not that we have to tell everything, or tell it all at once, or even know beforehand all we need to tell. But an honorable relationship is one in which we are trying all the time to extend the possibilities of truth—and life—between us. The point is not merely to get what we want (although that may very well happen). The goal of truth-telling is greater personal integrity and wholeness, life-giving intimacy with others, and the richness that comes when we accept the differences in experience that many people bring to our society, as well as to the body of Christ.

There is a power that comes from saying what we believe and believing what we say. This is the strength we have to offer our world. When we give that up, we become fragmented at our very core. It is painful and exhausting for a woman to begin to uncover the truth of her own experiences in a culture that has assigned more importance to what men think, feel and say. But the relationships, the Christian communities and the social and political structures worth having require that we engage in this difficult yet rewarding process. As women of integrity, we cannot settle for anything less.

Spiritual Exercises

Alone with God

Silence. As you come to the end of this chapter, take a few moments to sit with God in the silence of your heart.

- Is there an area in your life where you know a truth needs to be told—within yourself, in your relationship with God, in your relationship with others?

- Where do you play games with truth rather than walking freely in truth?

Do not feel as if you have to do anything with the truth that you just identified. Don't jump to any conclusions about the implications of telling this truth. Just sit with the truth in God's presence and allow yourself all the thoughts and emotions that come. As you sit with this truth, do you have any glimpses of the kind of freedom that might be waiting on the other side of your willingness to walk in this truth?

Prayer and journaling. Review the chapter that you have just read, noticing the places of resonance and resistance that you have highlighted. In your journal, tell God about the thoughts, feelings, desires and questions that this chapter has raised for you. Notice the places where your experiences and questions were the same as or different from the women described here. In your journal, express your feelings as well as your arguments and places of agreement or disagreement.

Invitations. God, are there any areas of my life where you are inviting me to walk more freely in truth? (As you ask God to invite you into truth, you might be thinking about the potential risks of truth-telling. You could express those concerns to God in prayer. You may also want to think about the potential rewards of truth-telling. Allow these to inspire you to do what you need to do.)

CHAPTER   FIVE

Escaping the Tyranny of the "Never-Enough" World

In the absence of other solid sources of identity, we are glad to root it in
our purchases. I shop, therefore I am.

MIKE STARKEY, *BORN TO SHOP*

When my husband and I were first married and living in a small apartment, I thought that if we could just buy a house I would be satisfied. We had married right out of college and started our family shortly thereafter, so the dream of owning a home seemed far off indeed. But miracles do still find their way into modern life: some acquaintances, who needed to quickly sell a home they owned, offered to help us with the down payment. Consequently, we became proud homeowners much sooner than we had expected. Even though it was a modest three-bedroom ranch in need of decorating and repair, it felt so good to have space! To walk out our front door into a grassy yard rather than a dank hallway seemed like heaven on earth. For the privilege of owning a home I could live with peeling paint, yellow and green wallpaper, and an outdated kitchen.

Or could I?

It didn't take long for me to realize that I'm not that easily satisfied. I was fine as long as the first flush of purchasing excitement lasted. But pretty soon, desire began to overtake me again. If we could just replace the shag carpeting, get rid of those avocado-colored appliances and remodel the kitchen, then I'd be satisfied.

Well, ten years later we had done all those things (and more!), and I had a startling realization: it doesn't matter how much we buy, there is always plenty more I want. The pull of things in my life is so deep and so strong that at times I have despaired of ever being free of it. I am very much a part of the "never-enough" world, and chances are, so are you. Do you ever wonder why, even though you understand the dangers of debt, you spend money that you don't have? Or why, when you are lonely or depressed, it seems to help to go shopping? Why, before the paint is even dry on one remodeling project, you are plotting the next one? Why you feel so much more credible when you're wearing full makeup and a business suit than when you're wearing a jogging suit and the face God gave you? Or why your husband feels that he can never satisfy your material wants? Do you ever wish for the freedom of being content with what you have? I wonder about myself sometimes, especially when my daughter once commented (with a perception beyond her years), "Daddy works so Mommy can buy the things she wants."

ALWAYS CONSUMING, NEVER SATISFIED

There are reasons that, with all that we have, it seems there are so many more things we just can't live without. In the never-enough world, the twin gospels of materialism and consumerism are preached nearly every time we open a magazine, turn on the television or talk to a neighbor. Materialism lulls us into believing that the physical, material world is the most "real," while consumerism, the dominant economic theory in North America, entices us with the idea that the accumulation of more and better things is a worthy goal for our lives. Mix in a little bit of spiritual or psychological flavoring and you get the idea that material things provide the answers to life's basic questions:

- *What am I worth?* The most expensive hair color product.
- *What is success?* Being able to buy dinner for my husband with my own credit card.
- *How do I find peace of mind?* Buy more insurance.
- *How do I show someone how much I love them?* Send them "the very best" greeting card.
- *What do I do when the going gets tough?* Go shopping, of course.

Materialism and consumerism dovetail in their promises that if we can just achieve a higher income level, get our dream house, wear the right clothes and enjoy the right leisure activities, we will be satisfied. But these two outlooks often produce families that are unable to get off the treadmill because they are deeply in debt . . . parents who have no time for each other or their children . . . families with nicer things than their parents had at that age but little time to enjoy them . . . men and women who know how to dress for success but are full of doubts and questions. Alongside our many acquisitions exists a profound sense of dissatisfaction that is never quelled for very long.

In *The Hidden Persuaders,* Vance Packard documents the way Americans are programmed to "consume, consume, consume, whether we need or even desire the products almost forced upon us." He observes that after World War II American manufacturers were able to produce many more goods than people were consuming, so they began exploring the question, "How can we stimulate the American people to buy more?"

They engaged sociologists and psychologists to teach them how to stimulate consumer buying by creating wants in people that they didn't realize existed. These trainers, who called themselves "motivation researchers," taught merchandisers to probe people's subsurface desires, needs and drives in order to find their points of vulnerability. What the merchandisers identified were the very deepest human longings: our longings for love, our dreams of fitting in and "being somebody," our desire for power, and our need for emotional security. "Once these points of vulnerability were isolated, the psychological hooks were fashioned and baited and placed deep in the merchandising sea for unwary customers."

The way they began to hook us was to offer considerably more than the actual item involved.

A car becomes more than just a car; it becomes an expression of your truest self. A particular hair-coloring product becomes more than a beauty product; it tells me how much I'm worth. An exotic vacation becomes more than some needed rest and relaxation; it becomes the panacea for all relational ills. A certain beverage becomes more than just a way to quench one's thirst; it promises adventure and maybe even some "community" in the midst of the adventure. Obviously, these manufacturers are trying to sell us much more than a car or a beauty product or a beverage; they are "selling to our hidden needs" quite unashamedly.

Lack of contentment is now a part of the American cultural fabric. Manufacturers depend on the consumer (you and me) to be dissatisfied so that we will buy more and thus stimulate the economy. As one ad executive proclaims, "What makes this country great is the creation of wants and desires, the creation of dissatisfaction with the old and outmoded." So if you are dissatisfied, it is a sure sign that you were born in the U.S.A.!

GREAT EXPECTATIONS

Not only do hidden messages from our culture influence us, but the generation we belong to influences us as well. With the baby-boomer generation came a propensity toward an attitude of entitlement that has influenced us all. Researcher Landon Jones comments on this relatively new phenomenon: "For most of human history, people had thought that life was hard, brutal and tragic. The baby boom's early affluence [in the postwar years of the 1950s and 1960s] developed within it what some have called 'the psychology of entitlement.' What other generations had thought privileges, the baby boomers thought were rights."

I certainly see myself fitting into that description. I expected our "starter home" to be just that—a steppingstone along the way to something bigger. When we ended up living there much longer than I expected (fifteen years to be exact), I had to ask myself, *Who says?* People all over the world and in our own inner cities live with their extended families in small apartments. They never "expect" even to own a home, let alone the roomy suburban home that I and many of my fellow baby boomers have our hearts set on. Who says life owes that to me?

The generation younger than baby boomers, often called Generation X, is now in its twenties and thirties. As this generation seeks business success and family stability, they, too, hunger for the money and possessions that my generation wanted. Although younger generations often emphasize values other than money, we all find ourselves greedy at times for what we think is rightfully ours.

The more we understand the messages of consumerism and materialism, the more we are able to spot their lies and free ourselves from their tyranny. Rather than being manipulated by these messages on a subconscious level, we will be able to recognize them and get to the underlying facts. Only then are we in a position to make real choices.

BEWARE OF DANGER

Remaining unaware of the undercurrent of materialism can be dangerous. The most obvious danger is that the undercurrent can pull us into its powerful undertow before we even know it. Consider the biblical story of Lot's wife, a woman who was so attached to her things that it spelled major disaster for her and her family. Although we don't know much about her spiritual sensitivities, we do know that Lot was a godly man whose soul eventually grew deeply disturbed by the filthy lives of the Sodomites. But he was a soul divided. Even though he was deeply disturbed by what was going on around him, "he liked the good life of Sodom's society. He preferred making money off its citizens to staying in the hills where there would be no filthy living but also no 'good life.'" But he had a terrible price to pay for this indulgence. Rather than acting as an influence for good, Lot lost his own moral moorings, and God had to send two angels to forcibly lead Lot and his family out of Sodom before it was destroyed by the consuming fire of God. They literally grabbed Lot, his wife and their two daughters by the hands and physically forced them to leave, warning them in no uncertain terms, "Flee for your life; do not look back or stop anywhere in the Plain; flee to the hills, or else you will be consumed" (Genesis 19:17).

As the family hurried to safety, Sodom and Gomorrah and the entire plain in which these cities were located were consumed by fire and sulfur. And Lot's wife, trailing behind, looked back and was herself overtaken by sulfurous vapors. Encrusted with salt, she died there on the plain, captured in the pose that symbolized her attachment to the wealth, society and sin that had been her whole life.

We are not left to wonder about what was in the heart of Lot's wife that day. Christ himself interprets this story for us. When teaching his disciples about the coming of the kingdom of God, he warns them about being so caught up in the material world that they lose touch with spiritual realities. As an example, he mentions the people living in Lot's day, specifically Lot's wife:

> Just as it was in the days of Lot: they were eating and drinking, buying and selling, planting and building [in other words, completely caught up in the material world], but on the day that Lot left Sodom, it rained fire and sulfur from heaven and destroyed all of them—it will be like that on the day that the Son of Man is revealed. On that day, anyone on the housetop who has belongings in the house must not come down to take them away; and likewise anyone in the field must not turn back. Remember Lot's wife. (Luke 17:28-32)

Christ instructed the disciples to remember Lot's wife as an example of one whose attachment to material things had anesthetized her to spiritual realities. She had lived for physical realities for so long that she was unaware of the decay in her soul. Even when she came face to face with impending doom, she was unable to disentangle herself from the hold that the material world had on her heart. Her treasures were in Sodom, and with them her loyalty and affection. So she looked back, and it spelled her destruction.

It would be tempting to distance ourselves from this woman with protests like "I don't know her. I don't understand her. I would never . . ." But we do know her; she is our sister, and we have the same tendency to be deeply enamored with the things that we can see and physically know. Our doom may not be as sudden or dramatic as hers, but we are in just as much danger.

As one more contemporary woman laments, "Credit ruined my marriage, my self-image, and our family's future. It was a dreadful spiral that almost led to the loss of our home." She first applied for credit to pay off her overspending on Christmas presents. She was amazed at how easy it was to obtain credit and how accommodating the company was in hiding the loan from her husband: "Not only did I get it (cash in hand the following day!) but they also agreed to use my office address rather than my home address, so the deception began. From time to time they offered me further funds, which I was too weak to refuse, and I had by that time also contracted with various stores for credit card debts as well. Soon it was completely out of control, and I had to borrow further just to meet monthly payments."

The worse the problem became, the harder it was to tell her husband the truth; it was only when she was close to a mental breakdown that the truth came out. In her desperation, she turned to her church, where the pastor and treasurer took charge of their finances. Although they were able to negotiate a workable repayment schedule with her creditors, she had at least ten years of repayment ahead of her. However, the worst part was the damage this situation caused to her relationship with her husband. In her own words, "The most awful thing to deal with is the lack of trust and forgiveness toward me by my husband, but who can blame him? Debt turned me from an honest trustworthy person into a deceitful liar. . . . Whatever I hear about people's shortcomings these days, my reaction is 'there but for the grace of God go I.' It's so easy to fall into the debt trap."

This woman's story speaks to some of the most obvious pitfalls in a materialistic society: debt and the accompanying rat race, loss of integrity and fractured relationships. Our human desire for more things and nicer things coupled with our existence in a society that encourages us to "buy now, pay later" is a highly combustible combination. There but for the grace of God go many of us—and some of us are already teetering right on the edge of financial disaster.

OUR EMPTINESS OF SOUL

But other dangers lurk beneath the shimmering surface of the material sea. They are harder to spot, to be sure, but they are no less real.
What I've noticed about myself is that when I get too caught up in
the constant noisiness of day-to-day activity and purchasing, my soul
becomes numb. The stillness in which the voice of God can be heard
never comes. The truth that is born of quietness and expectant waiting is lost in the din of a frantic world. The opportunity to spend my
life for a cause that is greater than myself is forfeited when I keep
grabbing for things that will give me instant but short-lived gratification. It's a vicious cycle: The more I give myself over to the material
world, the emptier I feel inside. The emptier I feel, the more I am attracted to things that will distract me from those feelings. The more
distracted I am from the emptiness I'm feeling, the less opportunity
there is to fill it with what is truly satisfying. Even when I know that
more commitments and more spending are not good for me, I'm not
always able to say no.

While it is sobering to face the fact that there are areas in our lives
that are out of control, this realization gives us the needed motivation
to quiet ourselves and ask crucial questions. Often the questions we
are willing to ask ourselves are just as important as the answers we
think we know. Questions such as these:

- What do I expect out of life, and where do those expectations
  come from?

- What is success, and do I tend to measure it by outward trappings?

- How much of myself am I giving to my loved ones, and how much
  am I relying on expensive gifts to communicate love?

- What is happening inside me and in my relationships right before
  I go on an unnecessary shopping spree?

- What happens for me when I do let things get quiet? Is it peaceful, or is there unresolved pain that surfaces?
- What is the real source of the emptiness or drivenness that I feel?

In the noisiness of our lives, it is hard to quiet down and wait for the answers to questions as important as these. The truth that has come in my own quiet listening is this: As much as I am influenced by the tide of cultural messages, the source of my discontent goes far deeper than that. In the quietness I have found a woman who has often allowed the affluence of her community to shape her expectations and feed her dissatisfaction. I have found a woman who can be unsure of her worth when she is not achieving. A Christian who knows how to do all the "Christian stuff" but has a lot to learn about being still and being utterly satisfied in the presence of God. A wife who finds it much easier to buy things for her husband than to offer unconditional love, acceptance and affection. A mother who has let her children slip into the same frantic pace to which she is so prone, rather than building a life for them in which the material world is balanced with relationships, participation in the work of family life, and quiet time for reading, reflection and cultivating spiritual awareness.

These are the places where I have needed to start stemming the tide of materialism in my own life. As I have learned to receive God's unconditional love for me and embrace the beauty of who I am as a created being uniquely called by God, as I have experienced the soul satisfaction of giving more of myself to the people I love, as I have worked with the structure of our family life to include more of what matters most, as I have spent more time quietly in God's presence (not doing, just being), the pull of the material world has begun to lessen.

REAL ANSWERS

In some ways it would be easier if someone would just come along and tell us exactly how much is enough so that we could fall into line. But answers that fit into simple categories of right and wrong or 1-2-3 solutions are not real answers. Neither are answers that hold up someone else's lifestyle for us to copy. These rob us of the opportunity to stop our material madness long enough to experience the empty places in our soul—the insecurity that is masked by all those "dress for success" clothes, the disappointment of an unfulfilling marriage that is numbed by constant activity, or the depression that is kept at bay by the rush we get when we go shopping. Only when we have quieted ourselves long enough to listen to what is happening within us do real answers begin to emerge.

WE MAY TRY TO FILL OUR EMPTINESS BY ACQUIRING MORE THINGS. BUT THERE WILL NEVER BE ENOUGH MATERIAL THINGS TO SATISFY THE LONGINGS OF THE HUMAN SOUL.

The truth is that we are created to be in relationship with God and others in ways that fill our soul. Just as our individual hereditary characteristics are embedded in our chromosomes, so our need and ability for relationship is embedded in the DNA of our soul. When sin, rebellion or lack of attention causes rifts in our most important relationships, the emptiness of soul that results can be very painful. We may try to fill our emptiness by acquiring more things. But there will never be enough material things to satisfy the longings of the human soul. That is why Hebrews 13:5 draws such a strong connection between freedom from materialism and our relationship with God: "Keep your

lives free from the love of money, and be content with what you have;
for [or because] he has said, 'I will never leave you or forsake you.' "

The questions that materialism claims to answer are important indeed, but the answers can be found only in a personal relationship
with God that is growing deeper every day. *What am I worth?* I am
worth so much that God sent his Son to experience the pain of sin
and then take my penalty. *What is success?* Truly knowing God and accomplishing his purposes for my life. *How do I find peace of mind?* In
knowing that God will never leave me. *How do I show someone I love
them?* By giving myself sacrificially as Christ did. *And what do I do
when the going gets tough?* I place my confidence in a loving God who
has promised to help.

The real questions help us acknowledge the emptiness of soul that
makes us vulnerable to the hooks embedded in the messages of our
culture. Real answers offer insights about ourselves, the material
world and the spiritual world that free us to choose a lifestyle consistent with our core values rather than cultural norms. Real answers
help us keep our perspective in a world where desire is out of control.
Real answers take us deeper into the relationships for which we were
created. Real answers are found in becoming more consistent and intentional about pursuing those relationships. Over time, almost im-
perceptibly at first, we become less obsessed with money and things
and begin finding true satisfaction for the empty places of our soul.

KEEPING THINGS IN PERSPECTIVE

I would be unrealistic if I did not admit how much I enjoy the things
money buys. Our home with its grassy lawn and good neighbors has
been a wonderful place to raise our family and host our friends. The
"sacred space" where I write and receive people in spiritual direction
has become a true haven for prayer and listening for God's voice.

Money spent on trips and vacations has been money invested in relationships, soul care, and appreciation of our created world. And life would certainly be more difficult without adequate, regular income. I enjoy these gifts without guilt because God "richly provides us with everything for our enjoyment" (1 Timothy 6:17).

But a balanced perspective reminds me that money does have its limitations. It can buy clothes but not confidence, cosmetics but not true beauty, an exotic vacation but not the ability to relax and sleep. Money provides alarm systems but not peace of mind, a shopping trip but not a friend to go with you, a *Better Homes and Gardens* house but not a mom who has time and energy left to play games or read stories. It buys expensive gifts but not love.

A balanced perspective also keeps me from being consumed by my materialistic desires and warns me about sacrificing what really matters for things that never quite satisfy. The material world offers a lot to women today—jobs, titles, sophisticated clothes, beautiful houses. It's tempting to try to grab for it all at once. But there is great potential for regret in this area, potential for getting to the end of our lives and realizing, *I put so much pressure on my husband (or myself) to make more money or go into more debt that the rat race damaged our relationship.* Or, *We got our dream house and car, but I had to go to work to pay for it all. I missed being home with my kids during the times they needed me most.*

Contrary to the messages of materialism, it isn't the woman who dies with the most toys who wins. Freedom from the tyranny of the never-enough world comes in wanting only what you have rather than being driven to acquire everything you want. As we grow more contented with what God has given us, rather than straining for what he has not given, we are less vulnerable to the dangers of debt, the demands of a consumerist culture and the emptiness of soul that keeps us striving for more. As we learn to allow our relationship with God and with others to satisfy the emptiness of our soul, the hooks embedded within our materialistic culture can no longer find a place inside us to attach themselves to. And then we are free indeed!

SPIRITUAL EXERCISES

Alone with God

Silence. As you come to the end of this chapter, take a few moments to sit with God in the silence of your heart and ask, *Which of the dangers associated with the material world am I most vulnerable to right now?* Without feeling like you have to do anything, allow yourself to notice the ways in which this vulnerability plays out in your life.

Prayer and journaling. Review the chapter that you have just read, noticing the places of resonance and resistance that you have highlighted.

- Where in your life right now do you get hooked by cultural messages?

- Are you able to recognize those times when you use material things to distract you from your emptiness of soul?

- Which of the bulleted questions listed on page 101 do you recognize as questions you ask yourself?

Allow yourself time to journal your responses to these questions and to tell God what you are noticing about yourself in relation to the material world. Identify what you need most from him these days and then express your need to him in prayer.

Invitations. God, are you inviting me to do anything in response to what I have read today? How do you want me to respond to your invitation?

Cultivating a Marriage That Works

When I look at it [my wedding dress], it hurts that all that care is taken to
preserve a dress when so little care was taken to preserve a family, but I
guess its easier to store a dress than to make a marriage work.

PATTI ROBERTS

Marriage certainly does receive mixed reviews in contemporary culture. Women today run the gamut from pinning all our hopes on marriage to rejecting marriage as a trap that relegates us to limited roles and responsibilities. Bachelor and bachelorette parties traditionally given for grooms and brides on the eve of their wedding seem to reflect this tension. In many cases, the spouse-to-be commemorates a final night of "freedom" by watching raunchy movies and joking about the marriage trap, yet this is contradictory to the dreams many of us have about getting married.

Undoubtedly, many of society's images of married life—the nagging wife who lets herself go over the years, the couch-potato husband whose most effective communication is yelling for his beer, unruly kids, bills that never end, perfunctory sex—do perpetuate the idea that marriage is a trap. But in actuality most of us get married because we have great hope that our marriage will be one of the exceptions—one of the few that really work. Deep down, most of us do not believe that marriage is a trap; we believe the truth that marriage is given to be a source of great joy and fulfillment. Otherwise, we probably wouldn't even consider it!

Sometimes—when a marriage isn't working—it is experienced as a trap. This happens when conflicts are left unresolved, faulty communication patterns become entrenched, pain and hurt are stuffed down instead of dealt with, and fitting into traditional roles is more important than understanding individuals. When we feel trapped, we have a tendency to feel desperate. And desperation can tempt us to ease the pain of a marriage that isn't working by getting involved with someone else, physically leaving the marriage or shutting down emotionally. However, in a marriage that is working there is great freedom: to love and be loved, to allow ourselves to be transformed in the context of a committed relationship, and to support each other in finding the truest expression of our most authentic selves.

So what does "a marriage that works" look like?

A MARRIAGE THAT WORKS FREES BOTH THE WIFE AND THE HUSBAND TO CONTINUE TO DISCOVER WHO THEY ARE AND TO FUNCTION AS A TEAM ACCORDING TO THEIR GIFTS, PERSONALITIES AND STRENGTHS.

A MARRIAGE BIG ENOUGH FOR BOTH OF US

A marriage that works frees both the wife and the husband to continue to discover who they are and to function as a team according to their gifts, personalities and strengths. Preconceived notions about

male-female roles in marriage have the potential to thwart this process of discovery and teambuilding, putting people in boxes so small
that real persons cannot fit into them!

Listen in on Diane's story of a marriage in which there is a lot of
room for her husband and very little room for anyone else:

> I became a submissive wife [as a means of] survival. It meant
> learning to live and survive in peace and getting as much my
> way as I could, without causing a lot of commotion. I would
> have to calculate: Clifford will only let me have my way on so
> many things within the next week, so I'd better decide what
> those things are going to be. I gave up some things for myself—
> personhood things—so the girls could have more. . . . I had
> stamina enough to fight for what the girls needed, but not
> enough left over to get what I needed. It meant a lot of manip-
> ulation and very little confrontation. . . . I know it wasn't
> healthy for me. After several years of this I began having all sorts
> of physical symptoms, and I think they're related to the stress
> that this submission caused. But I don't see any other way I
> could have done it. Clifford is just too strong of a person for me.

Clearly Diane's marriage isn't working at some very deep levels,
leaving both her and her husband extremely vulnerable. Diane is vulnerable to emotional and physical breakdown, to falling for the first
man who comes along and treats her kindly, to getting to the point
someday where she says, "I've had it up to here and I'm leaving!" Clifford is vulnerable to the boredom that comes from living with a
woman who has lost herself and her vitality because she has given
most of it away for so long.

While it may seem easiest to take the path of least resistance and
allow the more dominant partner to take over in the marriage, culti-

vating a male-dominated marriage is actually very detrimental to the husband-wife relationship over the long haul. When a woman surrenders her personhood—her thoughts, her opinions, her personality, her decision-making prerogative—to her husband, she has less to bring to the relationship. While she might seem compliant and content, as time goes by she becomes more and more dependent on her husband until sometimes it seems like she is barely there! Eventually, as she becomes more aware of how much of herself she has given up, powerful feelings of loss and resentment begin to well up—against her husband, God and anyone else she feels is responsible for such an unfair system. She begins to feel trapped and becomes vulnerable to anything or anyone that promises freedom.

The situation worsens as the husband continues to develop himself through his work and other outside contacts while the woman may not feel as free to pursue her goals, dreams and personhood. In such a situation, the husband may begin to outgrow his wife and become bored with her or grow away from her and feel that she is no longer a capable friend and confidante. This becomes a vicious cycle: the woman keeps trying to fulfill her role as the adoring, caring wife, but the husband is now wanting something else. He may be embarrassed by what she has (or, more accurately, *hasn't* become) and resentful that she has not kept up. Experiencing guilt about the way he feels, he may continue to pamper or coddle her to make himself feel better about the whole situation. Or he may succumb to an affair, or he may even just leave the marriage—in what feels like a sudden turn of events but, in actuality, has been on the way for a long time.

In Diane's situation, she isn't doing herself, her husband or her children any favors by maintaining the status quo of a marriage that isn't working. In fact, by working so hard to fit into a dysfunctional family system, she is actually helping to perpetuate it and pass it on to future generations. She needs to consider whether God is calling her to lead the way into "the tunnel of chaos" in order to move toward a marriage that is really working rather than one that just looks good from the outside.

Of course, dysfunction can go the other way too—a wife who becomes dominant while her husband becomes more and more distant from his partner and their children. Most of us have known families in which the husband spends most of his time in the garage or basement puttering, or sitting at a bar with people who give him a sense of importance and belonging, or glued to the television in numbed silence. Meanwhile, the wife runs the household, brings up the children, decides the social agenda and frequently verbalizes what she sees to be her husband's weaknesses. Men aren't the only ones with strong personalities that can crush the life out of a relationship when left unchecked. A male-dominated marriage may be more common, but imbalance in either direction is unhealthy and not the plan God ever had for marriage.

Nourished by love. Scriptural instruction on marriage is grounded in the context of mutual submission among believers who are bearing with one another, forgiving each other, loving each other, telling each other the truth, and teaching and admonishing each other with thankful hearts in the name of Christ. This is a far cry from the "submission for the sake of survival" that has Diane tiptoeing around a man who does a lot of taking and very little giving.

The biblical concept of headship is modeled on the example of Christ's relationship with the church—not the hierarchy of corporate America with its presidents and vice presidents. According to Ephesians 5:22-33, Christ's role as "head" of the church involves being her Savior (giver of life), lover (to the point of laying down his life) and nurturer (caring for her as he would care for his body). Contrary to some interpretations, headship has nothing to do with demanding obedience, being the one who makes final decisions, or being the one who pursues his calling while the wife tries desperately to be supportive and fit in. Rather, the word *head* is virtually synonymous with "beginning" or "origin." In the context of Christ, the church and marriage, headship has to do with being the one who initiates and leads the way in loving. The woman responds (as the church does) to this kind of love with a heartfelt desire to please her husband.

Gilbert Bilezikian states in his careful word study:

> The concept of headship in the New Testament refers to the function of Christ as the fountainhead of life and growth and to His servant role of provider and sustainer. . . . Because Christ is the wellspring of the church's life and provides it with existence and sustenance, in return the church serves Him in loving dependency and in recognition of Him as the source of its life. Because man as the fountainhead of the woman's existence was originally used to supply her with her very life, and because he continues to love her sacrificially as his own body in marriage, in return a Christian wife binds herself to her husband in a similar relationship of servant submission that expresses their oneness. The imposition of authority structure upon this exquisite balance of reciprocity would paganize the marriage relationship and make the Christ/church paradigm irrelevant to it.

Two individuals love and give to each other in such a way that both souls are nourished. A husband commits himself to love, nurture and see that his wife has what she needs to be all that she is meant to be—to the point of laying down his own comfort, indeed his very life. The wife gives to her husband out of the fullness that comes from being truly loved and nurtured into full personhood.

Their balance and unity speak volumes to a world burdened with trying to find love in relationships fraught with domination, manipulation, power struggles and selfishness.

Exploring the possibility of unity. But what about those times when you and your husband just can't agree? Many couples have been taught that in such moments the husband should be the one to make the decision; nothing in Scripture supports this idea. Rather, the Scriptures speak of unity as the goal for relationships among Christians, married or otherwise: "Be of the same mind, having the same love, being in full accord and of one mind. Do nothing from selfish ambition or conceit, but in humility regard others as better than yourselves. Let each of you look not to your own interests, but to the interests of others" (Philippians 2:2-4). This is the norm for Christian marriage.

How many decisions come along that are truly worth sacrificing the powerful unity that I have discussed so briefly here? How many are so important that we cannot wait for each other and listen and work lovingly to achieve the one mind spoken of in Philippians 2:3-5? My husband and I haven't yet come up against a decision that was worth such a sacrifice.

The rush to designate the husband as the one who makes the final decisions is rooted in simple fear—fear that unity and consensus is not possible. Fear that if we don't give more power to one or the other, we'll never be able to make decisions. Fear that if women are not kept in some sort of authority structure, they will lead their men and their families down the path to destruction. While such fears are understandable, they are woefully inadequate as a foundation for marital relations. They totally discount the efficacy of the Holy Spirit's work in creating unity among us. They discount the power of Christlike love and mutual submission.

Faith, on the other hand, holds out for God's ideal of agreement and oneness before moving ahead. Faith says, "I believe that unity is God's will for us, and he can bring our hearts and minds together."

Certainly, there are times when one spouse may say to the other, "You know what? I think this decision affects you more than it does me, so let's go your way on this one." But that is a concession voluntarily given, not forced upon another on the basis of gender or anything else. There is a world of difference between a marriage in which deference is freely given and one in which it is understood that the husband always holds the trump card in the nitty-gritty of decision making. There is a great difference between a marriage where issues are worked out in a reasonable way and one in which the husband is outwardly "head of the house" while his wife pulls all the strings through deception and manipulation.

A MARRIAGE FLEXIBLE ENOUGH TO ACCOMMODATE CHANGE

When Chris married me at twenty-one, he thought he was getting a traditional girl whose main goals in life were to be a good wife and mother. He thought that because that's what I told him! Can you imagine his surprise (and mine too) at finding out later that even though I treasured and valued my marriage and my children, I needed more? I discovered a great deal of fulfillment in work that involved leading causes that I was passionate about and providing spiritual guidance through speaking and writing. In fact, my desire to be involved in ministry was clarified and intensified at the same time that God was giving us children; our relationship had to stretch in order to accommodate these changes.

Neither of us could ever have envisioned the various configurations that have characterized our family life through the years. We have struggled to accommodate the ages and stages of our children in combination with our own different callings to contribute to the world beyond our home. At times we have appeared to be fairly traditional—Dad works while Mom stays home and makes childrearing her primary responsibility. The freelance nature of my work along with Chris's willingness to flex his hours and cover the home front when needed made this possible for a number of years.

Most recently, we have been engaged in a dual-career dance with both of us managing vocations to which we feel deeply called. Although our children are older now, we are still committed to being the primary influences in their lives and to having our home be a well-supervised and open environment for our children and their friends. Just as in the early years, our two-career home requires commitment to each other, to God's call on each of our lives, to creative and flexible thinking and problem solving, and a big dose of that indispensable "can do" attitude. Of course, now it does not just involve Chris and me, but all of us. We are learning what it means to be a family where each person's calling—Mom, Dad and children—is valued and supported.

This flexible kind of family life is not something that gets figured out once and for all, and then everything runs smoothly ever after. Rather, we are very much in process, working on things as we go, communicating honestly when things aren't right, brainstorming solutions and making adjustments as things change. We are accepting the fact that we're not perfect, but we love each other and want to celebrate what God is doing in and through each of our lives.

One creative solution that worked well for us was the time when we arranged for our sixteen-year-old daughter to cover the home front two days a week as part of her paid summer work. *She* suggested this as we brainstormed about how to handle the summer break with two parents needing to work outside the home at least part of the time. The variety of the tasks—cooking, cleaning, shopping, driving and overseeing the activities of two younger sisters— appealed to Charity's capacity for leadership and organization (more so than other summer jobs she could have held) and gave her valuable experience that will benefit her over the long haul.

The result of this creative solution? We would come home on the nights Charity had been in charge to find the house clean, dinner ready, two younger daughters who had done their chores and played with their older sister, and a sixteen-year-old who was tired but proud of her accomplishments. We were pleased at what God was doing in our family even though our lives seemed so complex and busy.

It is not always easy for families to stretch enough to accommodate a woman's calling to commitments beyond the home. It requires a significant amount of giving and taking on everyone's part. But as we continue to work toward an arrangement that fits who we are and who we are becoming, it is anything but stifling!

FACING PROBLEMS AND GETTING HELP

As a young woman preparing for marriage, I didn't realize that marriage would be hard and that it would take more than love and a commitment to Christ to make it work. Either no one was saying it or I just wasn't listening—probably a combination of both.

Now I know that most married couples (the honest ones anyway!) will sometimes encounter real marital difficulties: anger so deep that it cannot be fully dealt with "before the sun goes down," depression that cannot be lifted by one more sermon or book on victorious Christian living, sexual difficulties that are not alleviated by simplistic teaching about sex as God's beautiful gift, or a crisis that threatens to overwhelm them. I know this because Chris and I have experienced the kind of difficulties that have brought us to the point of saying, "Look, we have a problem. We have tried everything we know to try, and it's just not working. We need help."

It's a little traumatic at first—a real blow to your pride—to admit that you need help and then to seek it actively. Then there is the challenge of finding someone who has the expertise, experience and perhaps professional training to be of real help, and placing yourself in the position of being guided and helped. But the beauty of having a helper for times of stress in marriage is that the helper can become a kind of safety net as we move toward greater levels of intimacy in the relationship. Rather than being afraid of new awareness and new issues that need to be dealt with ("if I told my husband that I really don't like sex, he would be devastated"; "if I told my wife about my struggle with pornography, she would never forgive me"; "my husband would be revolted if I told him about my eating disorder"; "how can I tell my wife it really bothers me that she has let her appearance go?"), we can bring issues out into the open, knowing that there is someone to help if we get stuck or the problems become bigger than we know how to handle.

We all have unresolved issues that keep us from experiencing the fullness of life we have envisioned for ourselves. Much of the work of maturing and healing the hurts of the past can be done only in meaningful connection with another person over time. Dysfunctional thinking patterns, poor communication skills and character weaknesses don't change overnight or in isolation. The beauty of a marriage that works is that these areas are viewed matter-of-factly rather than as disasters that cannot be coped with. Marriage then becomes one of the contexts for God's transforming work in us.

Yes, pride does die hard. That's why some people wait until it hurts so badly they can't stand it or until some kind of crisis forces the issue. But in marriages that are working well, admitting problems honestly and getting help is seen as a strength and not a shortcoming. "Wisdom is with those who receive counsel" (Proverbs 13:10 NASB). The sooner the better.

LEARNING TO LET GOD BE OUR SOURCE

As a young wife I thought that somehow I could take away all of my husband's pain, that my answers would solve his problems, that I could fill up his empty places. And I expected that he would do the same for me. These expectations were draining because, in reality, only God can do those things.

In *Families Where Grace Is in Place,* psychologist Jeff Van Vonderen observes that much of the tiredness and "trappedness" that married people feel is a result of having the wrong job description. Many of us enter into marriage thinking that it is our job to meet each other's deepest needs. Inevitably, we both fail to live up to these expectations, and so we try to fix each other. The problem with fixing is that it just doesn't work, and pretty soon everyone ends up feeling like a failure—the "fixee" because he or she hasn't lived up to his or her spouse's expectation, and the "fixer" because he or she hasn't been able to effect change.

EVENTUALLY WE MUST FACE THE TRUTH THAT NO HUMAN BEING IS CAPABLE OF FILLING UP ANOTHER HUMAN BEING, NO MATTER HOW MUCH FIXING WE DO.

Eventually we must face the truth that no human being is capable of filling up another human being, no matter how much fixing we do. And we can't really change anyone but ourselves. I realize now that my "job" as a married woman is to keep learning to let God meet my needs and change my destructive behaviors. As I mature in my ability to deal with anger, communicate truthfully with love and respect, break annoying habits, and conquer my own selfishness, I find that I have much more to offer Chris. As I see more clearly what I can't do for him (fixing and filling), I am freed to offer what I am best equipped to offer: my presence on the journey, a listening ear, any tools or insights I have gained along the way, and my support and participation in wrestling with life's great questions.

Does this mean that we are not concerned about each other's needs? In a marriage that works, both the husband's and the wife's needs are very important. However, even as we express our deep care for one another, we are realistic about what one human being can do for another. We can love each other wholeheartedly, but that love cannot be expected to fill up the hole left by a mother or a father who could not love. One human being can be a source of deep joy to another but cannot single-handedly stave off depression. Being a husband or a wife can be a part of our identity for the time that God gives us to be together, but it cannot give ultimate meaning to our life. We can cultivate our sexual relationship, but we cannot accept responsibility for the other's choice if either one chooses to go outside the marriage for sexual fulfillment when the going gets tough. We can ease each other's pain with our presence, but we must each take responsibility for whatever work needs to be done in our own life—be it forgiveness, righting past wrongs, grieving loss or wrestling with God. Parts of the journey we each must take alone, and God is the only one who can go with us.

For those of us who are used to fixing and controlling, the idea of letting go of those responsibilities can be frightening. We may fear that our spouse or our marriage will never change unless we're right in the middle of things pushing, manipulating or giving advice! But faith can free us: faith in God's power to change people, faith in each other's capacity to change and faith in the whole process of being changed by marriage.

FREEDOM WORTH FIGHTING FOR

You have to choose your battles carefully. Some things are not worth doing battle over, but other situations call for all-out war. In a society that does little to promote faithful commitment to one spouse, the battle for our marriages is a battle worth fighting with every effective weapon we have.

Those of us who are willing to fight for the goodness that come in a healthy marriage will need to work at keeping our marriage fulfilling and fun. This means discovering the kinds of activities that we both find to be life giving and that we can enjoy doing together and then making significant time, energy and money available for them. We can also work at developing mutual interests so that the phenomenon of "creeping separateness"—the tendency to be so engrossed in our own activities and interests that we have less and less in common with our spouse—doesn't set in.

Stay alert to subtle dangers. Staying informed of societal trends helps us to be aware of subtle dangers to our marriages. A number of divorced male CEOs interviewed for a *Fortune* article indicated that while their first wife was "cold and unresponsive," their second wife was "supportive and sexy." The first wife was seen as unable to adjust to her husband's changing interests and unsupportive of the demands of his professional life, often becoming his self-appointed critic and conscience. In short, "she didn't keep up." While these are not acceptable excuses for a man to leave "the wife of his youth" it does make us aware of the need to be attentive to the quality of our presence with our husband and to the ways we can deepen the attraction that drew us together in the first place.

Be aware of yourself. We tend to assume that men are the only ones vulnerable to the temptation to betray the marriage relationship, but the truth is that women are vulnerable too. When our life is full of stress and we're seeking to meet everyone else's needs, attention and affirmation from a male friend or colleague can be all too attractive.

Self-awareness is the key here. It may be that one of the most important things a woman can do for her marriage is to be assertive enough to say, "Hey, I'm running on empty too much of the time—we need to make some adjustments." When a couple is serious about protecting their marriage, they assimilate this information and brainstorm ways to prevent the tiredness and emptiness (in the individual and in the marriage) that could leave the woman open to making a choice that she would later regret.

Keep talking. Even in good marriages, it is probable that a spouse will be attracted to someone else at some point. As difficult as it is to talk about this, these are the times when it is most important to keep talking—to keep telling the truth in love. Issues that we leave unacknowledged and unspoken have more power over us than those things we bring into the light.

A woman who faced the possibility of having an affair with a married Christian man reflects on her situation:

Although many things were strong in my marriage, there was not a real cherishing of each other. After so many years of marriage and so many children, maybe we were taking each other for granted. And here comes someone who opens my doors, and treats me with respect, and understands a lot about me. I could have done two things: I could have kept my temptation secret or I could have shared the whole thing with Chuck. I chose to tell my husband. And things really changed for us. We started spending more time together, we spent hours in the bedroom talking. . . . We came out with an appreciation for our relationship we hadn't had before. We realized that to lose what we had would be totally devastating.

Denying that we or our partner is vulnerable to outside attractions is just that—denial. While we may wish to spare each other information that is painful, such secrecy actually weakens the marriage (because we are hiding something important about ourselves), reduces opportunity for accountability and gives these attractions greater power over us.

An honest look at sexuality requires courage and a common commitment to increasing intimacy. The one doing the telling must communicate that he or she is doing so out of a commitment to honesty and a desire to protect the marriage. The one listening must work hard to articulate his or her honest response without punishing, controlling or withdrawing. Both should have the freedom to ask each other about outside attractions and to remind each other that honesty, faithfulness and true intimacy are among their highest shared values.

A BATTLE FOR THE BRAVE OF HEART

Sometimes when we experience the normal stresses and strains of becoming truly intimate with another person, we begin to believe that marriage is a trap. We begin to believe that if we could only get out of the marriage or try a new partner we would be a better person. The truth is that even if we got out of the marriage, we would still have to live with ourselves and those things in ourselves that keep us from joy, intimacy and effectiveness. We would still have to face those areas of ourselves that need to change. In most cases true freedom is still to be found in a marriage where we continue to change and transform, even through difficulty.

Fighting for the kind of a marriage relationship described here is not for the faint of heart. It is for hardy souls with courage enough to explore new frontiers and conquer the enemies of intimacy. It is for those who know deep in their heart that where there is no risk there is no reward. And it is for all of us who know what it is to push past our own limits of courage and strength, because, over time, a marriage that works provides a context and a catalyst for the transformation of growing souls.

SPIRITUAL EXERCISES

Alone with God

Silence. As you come to the end of this chapter, take a few moments to sit with God in the silence of your heart. If you are married, allow yourself to wonder, *Is my marriage a place of transformation these days? What's working in my marriage right now and what's not?* Without feeling as if you have to do anything about it, notice your longings, your joys, your questions about your marriage these days. If you are unmarried, reflect on the thoughts, feelings and questions you have about marriage. What can you do now to prepare wisely for a marriage that will be a place of continuing growth and transformation for you? What have you learned from married friends that will help you if and when you marry in the future? If you are single again due to divorce or the death of your spouse, reflect on your experience of marriage. How did your experience of being married transform (or deform) you? What worked? What didn't? Are there any unresolved issues that remain?

Prayer and journaling. Review the chapter that you have just read, noticing the places of resonance and resistance that you have highlighted. Allow yourself time to journal your response to the following questions and to tell God what's true about you and your marriage right now. Express to him your deepest desires.

- Where did you feel affirmed in something you were already doing or challenged to consider something new?

- Do any of the truths presented in this chapter invite you to embrace deeper levels of transformation than you are experiencing now?

- Do you feel hopeful or hopeless or something in between?

- If you are single or single again, what do you want to say to God about your present circumstances?

Invitations. God, are you inviting me to do anything in response to what I have read today? What is my response to you?

CHAPTER SEVEN

Embracing Our Sexuality

I praise you, for I am fearfully and wonderfully made.
  Wonderful are your works; that I know very well.

PSALM 139:14

On the eve of my wedding, a friend shared with me a great truth of human sexuality. She said, "You know, Ruth, before marriage the temptation is to have sex. After marriage, the temptation is not to."

At the time, I scoffed at this little bit of marriage wisdom. Now I realize that it does capture a dilemma in which many women find themselves. If a woman is a Christian or has spent time in and around the Christian community, she has been taught that sex is "God's wonderful gift" to be shared only with her husband in the context of marriage. So she spends the first part of her life slightly uncomfortable with her sexuality, waiting for it to find its full expression in marriage. But then she gets married and finds that it takes real intentionality to cultivate this important aspect of the human experience in the midst of the cares and concerns of life. What was meant to be a wonderful gift can begin to feel like a cruel hoax. Single women may wonder why they are so sexually alive when they can't express their sexuality fully; married women might find, over time, that they have become bored or disinterested. After some futile attempts to understand the forces at work, a woman may be tempted to dismiss the possibility of great sex as an unfortunate deception. But sex will not be dismissed that easily.

One can hardly pick up a book or magazine, watch television or a movie, or go to the mall or to the beach without encountering something that is intended to arouse us sexually. And unless we are completely unaware of it, our sexuality continues to call to us with inexpressible longing for more meaningful expression, for deeper connection with another human being. Each of us, married and single, is created by God as a sexual being; we have the potential to unite—body and soul—with another human being. That is the way God made us. The question is, how can we embrace the gift of our sexuality in whatever season of life we are in?

BEGINNINGS

The sexual journey begins long before we think of ourselves as being sexually awakened. It begins with all the early verbal and nonverbal messages that we received about our physical bodies generally and our sexuality more specifically. For many, feelings of shame, embarrassment or confusion regarding their sexuality go way back to messages they received about sex from their family of origin, the church, society, early sexual experiences and early experiences in marriage.

Perhaps sex was a taboo subject that made everyone uncomfortable, leaving children feeling ashamed of their natural curiosity about their bodies and their discoveries about sources of sexual pleasure. Others received verbal teaching that sex was good within marriage but received so many warnings about not falling into "sexual sin" that the whole thing seemed frightening and impossible to control. At the same time, they may have been observing a mother who pulled away from her husband whenever he tried to be physically affectionate or a father who grew distant from his daughters as they began to mature physically. And such *experiences* with sexual issues spoke louder than any verbal messages they were receiving. Still others received overtly negative messages about sex—it was bad, sinful, suspect or a duty to be endured.

In addition to the verbal and nonverbal messages we receive early on, certain kinds of experiences will shape us sexually. Early introduction into sexual activity by a family member, sexually arousing play with a member of the same sex, and sexual abuse are all experiences that influence who we become in terms of sexual knowledge and response. Sexual abuse, in particular, is much more prevalent than most of us realize. Healing the pain of sexual abuse is a process that takes time, willingness to tell the truth, and often expressions of anger and grief. For more insight into one woman's journey of healing from sexual abuse, see the endnote at the back of this book and pursue some of the other books listed in the resource guide.

One important aspect of the sexual journey, then, is to realize that each of us carries messages about sex from our early years as well as experiences that have shaped our attitudes about sex. Once we have taken an honest look at those early messages, we are able to decide, as adults, whether we agree with them. And once we have looked honestly at the experiences that shaped us, they no longer have so much power over the way we think and act. This kind of honest reflection can help us see how certain early experiences may be blocking or harming our present sexual functioning and our thoughts about our sexuality. As we look at ourselves and our development honestly, we can embrace what is good and true and move beyond what is no longer helpful. We can also become more aware and purposeful about what we communicate to the next generation about their sexuality.

The Sexual and Spiritual Connection

For many of us who grew up in and around the church, the relationship between sexuality and spirituality has been an uneasy one. Part of our religious heritage (at least for Protestant Christians and Catholics) has been "the sexless image of spirituality." At certain times in Christian history, true spirituality has been viewed as sexless, celibacy as the ultimate commitment to God, and bodily mortification and pain as conducive to spiritual purification. Women, the object of men's sexual yearnings, became particularly suspect in their sexuality. St. Thomas Aquinas stated, "God foresaw that woman would be an *occasion* of sin to man. Therefore he should not have made woman."

Fortunately, the church has begun to offer clearer thinking on sexuality, recognizing that it was created "good" and continues to be good. Particularly during the last couple of decades, we have witnessed a shift away from the overtly negative views driven by fear and thinly veiled disgust. Yet despite what (in many churches) amounts to a few statements about "God's wonderful gift of sex," discussion of topics related to sexuality are conspicuous by their absence. One notable exception is the annual "sex talk" for young people, when a pastor or youth worker gives instruction about sexual abstinence. Although abstinence is an important subject, it fails to address many other facets of sexuality. It's clear that despite some progress in this area, many Christians are still exceedingly uncomfortable with open discussion of sexual topics, especially in the context of their faith community.

Discomfort with matter-of-fact discussions of sexuality is due in part to a view that has remained strong in the church: the view that makes sharp distinctions between body and spirit and elevates the spirit as superior. This dualistic outlook causes us to avoid whole areas of life that are important parts of God's design for creation. Yet the Christian church suffers just as much as the rest of society from problems related to sexuality—teenage pregnancy, sexual abuse, troubled marriages—and we need to deal with sexuality openly, positively and systematically within the church, just as it would any other part of the Christian experience. Only by doing this can we learn to integrate the sexual and spiritual parts of our lives as the healthy combination God intended.

The need to think spiritually about sex. We've all heard the saying that the biggest sex organ is the brain. It's true! What we think and feel about sex probably has a greater effect on our sexual functioning than anything else. The problem is that many women *think* on an intellectual, rational level that sex is good, but they still *feel* uncomfortable with it. Exposing some of the early, faulty messages we received about sex will help with these uncomfortable feelings. It is also crucial that we gain a more accurate understanding of what God thinks about sex.

The foundation for embracing our sexuality more wholeheartedly can be found in the creation story, where we are told that "the man and his wife were both naked, and were not ashamed" (Genesis 2:25). The fact that their sexual parts were exposed was as comfortable for them as the fact that they had bare feet! They knew none of the shame and discomfort that are so prevalent today. For Adam and Eve in their sinless state, sexuality was a wonderful reflection of God's image, as were other aspects of their created being. Any discomfort they would later develop with their bodies and their sexuality was a direct result of their sin and the shame it introduced ("I was afraid, because I was naked; so I hid," Genesis 3:10).

Another reason why it is hard to think spiritually about sex is the lack of reverence and understanding that is created by the overexposure of sexuality in our culture. Sexuality is so routinely exploited in the media that nothing is off limits in terms of what is discussed and portrayed. Reality television has created a voyeuristic society in which even the most private human interactions are now lived out in front of a camera so that it can be broadcast to an audience. Nothing is preserved as private or sacred. As a result many people have become somewhat numb to the whole thing—completely out of touch with the spiritual as the relational significance of sexuality in general and sexual acts in particular.

Just recently, there was a news story about two fifth grade "couples" who started having sex in front of the class when their teacher left the classroom. Of course, the police were called and the matter was dealt with decisively, but it would be naive for us to ignore the fact that this incident is merely a surface manifestation of a much deeper issue. Normal fifth graders do not know how to have sex. Most fifth graders who are developing at a normal pace think the sexual act is gross. Obviously these children were mimicking adult sexual behaviors that they had probably witnessed many times in the media. In another place and time, fifth graders would not have been exposed enough to adult sexual activity to know how to mimic it.

Today a whole generation of young people has grown up influenced by overexposure to sexual activity as it is portrayed very explicitly in programs like *Dawson's Creek*, *Friends* and *Grey's Anatomy* to name a few. Before they have adequate filters in place, young people are imbibing a set of values that robs sexuality of its spiritual meaning by repeatedly presenting it as a recreational activity that is one among many possible activities that one can choose as part of a date. This cavalier view of sex fails to grapple with the fact that in

the act of sex two individuals become one flesh. The relational car-
nage that follows such a cavalier approach is profoundly damaging,
but the media certainly does not stop to make that point! All of us
are subject to the numbing affect and the disillusionment that results
from the disrespect and exploitation of sexuality that we witness on
a daily basis. As we learn to think spiritually about sex, we will need
to challenge not only our bad theology but also our current cultural
conditioning.

Looking back at Genesis, it is clear from this record of the earliest
days of human existence that the sexual side of ourselves cannot be
separated from the spiritual—together they make up who we are. To
try to compartmentalize the different aspects of ourselves leads to
confusion rather than spiritual health. From the creation story we
understand that maleness and femaleness and the dynamics between
the two are a work of God that he pronounced very good. The very
existence of the woman's clitoris is evidence that sex was given to us
for our enjoyment. Unlike any other body part, the sole purpose of
the clitoris is sexual pleasure.

Adam and Eve's comfort with their nakedness is a beautiful picture
of the openness and intimacy that are possible in marriage. The powerful experience of uniting one's body with another's is a physical
manifestation of the "one-fleshness" that God intended for the man
and woman who come together in mutuality and commitment. *God*
is the one who connects these sexual, relational and spiritual realities.

The need for reliable information. "I was very naive sexually when I
got married," says Nicolette.

> I wanted sex to be something wonderful, and it turned out to
> be a crock. It didn't stop hurting until after our first child was
> born. It sure wasn't fulfilling. I was on the pill. . . . I had no

knowledge that being on the pill is like being semi-pregnant, in
terms of hormones, and that being pregnant often brings a de-
crease in sexual interest. Nobody told me. I thought it was all
me. I thought something was wrong with me. I was a pretty re-
served person. . . . I *was* orgasmic once I got to the proper stage,
but I was never aroused before the encounter, and that seemed
like it would be so much fun! My hope was that I would be as
interested in sex as Dave was, that our appetites would be the
same. . . . All the time, I'd be thinking I've got to get better, I've
got to get better. But there was no better to get; I was really
stuck.

Nicolette's comments reflect a lack of information, which is a pre-
dictable result of our discomfort with speaking plainly about sexual
matters. Somehow moral people have developed an assumption that
if we do what is right and save ourselves for marriage, then everything will just fall into place when the time comes. While this may be
the case for some, most women benefit from having as much information as is available. The overexposure to sex in our culture is *not*
the same thing as having good, helpful information about how to cultivate a healthy approach to sexuality and intimacy over time.

All kinds of information would have been helpful to Nicolette and
her husband as they prepared for marriage and as they adjusted to
each other sexually after marriage—information about the mechanics of sex, the effects of birth control on sexual functioning, how female orgasmic response works, how best to communicate about sex,
and much more. Unfortunately, Nicolette had absorbed faulty information that had shaped her unrealistic expectations.

Ann, a vivacious and energetic woman in her thirties, describes
the problems misinformation caused in her sex life:

My husband and I were both virgins when we got married. We were very excited about our newfound sexual freedom and enjoyed our physical relationship immensely. I did not experience orgasm right away, but the closeness that we shared was so meaningful that I was not at all concerned. However, we were reading one of the few Christian sex books available at the time, which stated that simultaneous orgasm through intercourse was our "right" and we should pursue it. It also made a big distinction between "vaginal" orgasms and "clitoral" orgasms—vaginal orgasm (through intercourse alone) being the kind that mature women experience. Well, we bought into this idea hook, line and sinker until it began to rob us of the joy and uninhibitedness we had experienced early in our marriage. John started feeling pressured to produce such an orgasm, and I started feeling pressured to have one. The orgasms I was having regularly [through direct stimulation] suddenly seemed "less than." I felt like I wasn't a "real woman" yet.

Misinformation about female orgasmic response has been prevalent in our culture and has caused some couples to be overly focused on the woman achieving the "right" kind of orgasm—one experienced simultaneously with her husband during intercourse. As one woman said, "I finally had an orgasm, but my doctor told me it was the wrong kind."

Sigmund Freud in particular did a lot to propagate the "myth of the mutual orgasm." However, in their research Masters and Johnson found that all orgasms women experience involve the same physical components, from muscular contraction to a rise in heart rate and blood pressure. A woman's physiological response is the same regardless of what brings her to climax. This is not to say that there isn't any difference on an emotional level. Many women find that they enjoy different ways of experiencing orgasm at different times; it is purely a matter of personal preference, rather than a "right" and "wrong" way of doing things.

For Ann, this understanding was very freeing. "Sex became one big stress point," she says, "until we got more accurate information about the fact that most women need direct clitoral stimulation. . . . We read authors who encouraged us to relax and enjoy all the ways that we receive pleasure from being together. We're having a great time now that we're not so goal oriented."

MEN WANT IT, WOMEN DON'T (AND OTHER SEXUAL STEREOTYPES)

A stereotype is a conventional, formulaic and usually oversimplified conception of a person based on his or her sex, race, religion, ethnic background or other factors. Stereotyping on the basis of sex is so prevalent in our society that it is the relational air we breathe. Much of what we would like to call gender roles are just stereotypes, behaviors that we as a society have dubbed "normal" and "appropriate" over the years so that these behaviors have become widely accepted as the norm for human functioning. Some of the prevailing notions about men maintain that they are aggressive (or at least assertive), logical, unemotional, independent, dominant, competitive, objective, athletic, active and, above all, competent. Conversely, women are frequently viewed as passive, nonassertive, illogical, emotional, dependent, subordinate, warm and nurturing.

What is so striking about the above lists is that we all know many women and men who just do not fit them. That is the problem with stereotypes: they are simplistic, and they fail to take individuality into account, making life more difficult than it needs to be for the person who does not fit the stereotypes. Furthermore, acceptance of such narrow gender-role expectations can have a profoundly negative effect on our sexual functioning.

"Women are less interested in sex than men are." A common assumption in societies all over the world is that men's sexual desire is more powerful and regular than women's and that normal women simply don't enjoy sex as much as men do.

For the woman who is interested in sex and easily aroused, this stereotype can cause emotional ambivalence about her sexuality. She may have a hard time accepting her responsiveness as part of herself so that she can relax and enjoy sex as it is meant to be enjoyed. She may even begin to use her energies to block or hide her normal response rather than risk feeling like she is more interested or responsive than a "virtuous" Christian woman ought to be.

Joyce and Clifford Penner, respected Christian authors who have written about sexuality, describe the problem very well:

> The natural noises and behaviors typical of the sexual response cause in some women an inhibiting embarrassment that must be corrected. . . . As we—men and women—get aroused, we respond. Our heartbeat increases, we breathe faster and louder, we may experience muscular contractions, our bodies may feel like moving in thrusting or pushing motions, and we may have the urge to make gasping noises. Women who have difficulty allowing themselves to experience arousal or release are often unable to let themselves exhibit any or all of these behaviors. They are embarrassed and uncomfortable, and as with any other discomfort, they tend to avoid that which causes these negative feelings. Thus they will hold back their natural sexual responses.

If a woman continues to cut herself off from her sexual feelings, it will become a vicious cycle: as she distances herself from her sexual feelings, she will experience less pleasure, and when she experiences less pleasure, she will lose interest. Buying into the "men want it, women don't" stereotype (consciously or unconsciously) can inhibit a woman from fully experiencing the sexual nature God has given her.

"Men are the initiators and women are the responders." Unfortunately, this stereotype encourages women to be passive and allow themselves to be "acted upon" rather than actively seeking pleasure during lovemaking. In fact, being active and initiating at least some of the time is a key to enjoying the sexual experience fully. Scripture makes it very clear that sexual pleasure and release is a need for women as well as men and is equally important for both. "The husband should give to his wife her conjugal rights, and likewise the wife to her husband. For the wife does not have authority over her own body, but the husband does; likewise the husband does not have authority over his own body, but the wife does. Do not deprive one another except perhaps by agreement" (1 Corinthians 7:3-5).

Another natural result of our belief that men are to be competent leaders and women are to be not-so-competent followers is that men are expected to be "sexperts," which places an unnecessary burden on them. Rejecting this stereotype is helpful for men because sometimes they tire of being so responsible for the success of the sexual relationship. As one man says,

> Sometimes sex is more like work than fun. I have to make all the decisions—when and where we are going to have sex and what we are going to do together. It's my responsibility to make sure it works out good for both of us. This can put a lot of pressure on me and it gets real tiring always having to run the show.

It would be nice to have someone else call the shots for a change.

"Men cannot control themselves, so it is up to women to control them." This idea is particularly damaging to women. One of the strong messages many young girls receive as they grow up is that men are out of control when it comes to sex but that women can restrain them with proper feminine behavior and firm limits. Men, they are told, will "take as much as they can get," and so the woman must make sure that she is not coerced into unacceptable activities. For many young women, this comes to mean that if a man does show signs of interest or lust, or begins behaving inappropriately, it is somehow the woman's fault: she must not have been sitting properly, wasn't dressed discreetly enough, shouldn't have been so friendly, or *something*.

The natural result is that rather than feeling comfortable with her sexuality and accepting it as a natural part of life, a woman may experience an uncomfortable mixture of shame and pleasure surrounding it. Because of this ambivalence, she may increasingly distance herself from her sexual feelings and minimize any sexual feelings that others might have toward her.

A concern with control is not uncommon among adolescent girls during their dating years, and it can be effective in helping them not to compromise. But while there are some helpful elements to this stereotype (that's why stereotypes are so easy to fall into), sexuality is not a light switch that we can turn on and off at will. A woman who spends much time and energy regulating sexual intimacy to maintain her moral standards may have difficulty experiencing sexual feelings when it becomes appropriate for her to let go of those controlling behaviors in marriage.

We need to reject the idea that men cannot control their urges and therefore that women are responsible for them. On the contrary, men are just as capable of and responsible for controlling their own sexual urges as they are responsible for controlling any other urge, such as the urge to spend too much money, to overeat or to indulge in angry tirades. Yes, they have strong sexual desires and may be stimulated by what they see more than women are. Women do well to be sensitive to this. But we must not confuse sensitivity with responsibility.

A young girl needs to be encouraged to embrace her developing sexual interest and sensations as a part of what God created her to be, as cause for celebration of growth and life. Then when a young man experiences sexual desire for her, she will perceive it as evidence that everything is functioning as God intended, not that she has done something wrong. As we affirm how exciting and right it all is, we have the perfect opportunity to discuss the benefits of saving the fullest expression of our sexuality for the commitment and intimacy of marriage. Then when the time comes, there will be no need to turn the sexual switch from completely off to completely on. Rather, the sexual journey into marriage will be more like turning a dimmer switch from low to medium to high—a much more gentle transition.

WHAT SOME WOMEN HAVE LEARNED ABOUT SEXUAL SATISFACTION

Although lack of sexual fulfillment in marriage is very widespread, there is a significant percentage of married couples who are having good sex. And many single women, whether they have never married or are single again due to divorce or the death of a spouse, are able to embrace their sexuality. What might we learn from them?

LOVE AND SEXUAL INTIMACY CANNOT GROW IN A
GARDEN OF UNCERTAINTY.

Women who are enjoying their sex life know that great sex develops in a loving, committed relationship. Even though Chris and I have been married for many years, we still find new levels of intimacy to share. It would be very disturbing if, after a time of connecting at deep emotional and physical levels, he could walk away with a vague promise of "I'll call you sometime." For women in particular, love and sexual intimacy cannot grow in a garden of uncertainty.

Yet plenty of women are trying it the other way. Many single women are struggling to reconcile the strength of their sexual desires with the circumstances of their singleness in a society that throws sex in their face at every turn. Periods of singleness—which will come to all of us at one time or another—are enormously difficult in this regard. But if the sexual revolution taught us anything, it taught us that there are very good reasons for God's ideal of saving sexual intimacy for those who commit themselves to each other in marriage.

The words of a woman who tried it both ways are haunting in their description of our very real need for connection and of the disillusionment that comes from trying to meet it in the wrong way:

Sexuality mimics love. It compels tenderness and embraces, it forces the lovers to hug one another, to allay one another's pain through the revelations of sexuality, as when true love is exchanged. What follows such experiences? Disappointments, a bitter aftertaste, mutual accusations of bleak loneliness, feelings of exploitation and defilement. Neither of the two gave true love but only expected to receive it, therefore, neither received it.

Sex therapist Dr. David Schnarch proclaims, "The greatest sexual ecstasy comes not with a *Cosmo* cover girl, but with your spouse." He describes the electrifying sexual connection that can be reached by two people in a close, intimate relationship. He goes on to say that the reason many married couples don't achieve it is "because they are scared to reach their sexual potential within the overwhelming intimacy of marriage." Intensely intimate marital sex is more threatening than people realize, and it comes about only as couples "work past their fears and the discomfort that comes from breaking barriers of intimacy together." In other words, good marital sex happens only as we become increasingly "naked" in the presence of the other person and are not ashamed.

Women who are finding sexual fulfillment understand that the growth of a sexual relationship is not about technique but about two people learning how to be loving and intimate. They know it is a process complete with stops and starts, days when it seems like a lot is happening and days when it seems like nothing is happening. They accept the fact that there are obstacles to overcome, heights of ecstasy to be scaled and dry spells to wait through patiently. They understand that sexual freedom is not the freedom to have sex with anyone they want; it is the freedom to stay in the process of achieving true intimacy with another human being.

In addition, women who are experiencing sexual satisfaction do not worry about "how things ought to be." They are not agitating themselves with thoughts like *We should make love more often. I should be experiencing multiple orgasms. We should be trying this new position or that new toy.* Even though they seek help when they need it, they enjoy their sex life as uniquely their own and not to be compared with national averages or the latest magazine article. They accept the changes that different seasons and circumstances bring—pregnancy and childbirth, infertility, stress, work that requires travel for either partner, differing sexual appetites at different times, menopause, midlife crisis, aging. They do not view these as problems so much as opportunities to adjust, accept or search for new ways of loving.

A woman who is enjoying herself sexually is becoming increasingly at home in her body. In our culture, it is extremely difficult for a woman to feel good about her body. Anorexic actresses and models parade before us on television and in magazines, while images of women with various implants and plastic surgeries insist, *this* is what a sexual woman looks like!

All of us, when we compare ourselves to these images, feel inadequate in some way. Many of us bring negative feelings and images with us from growing-up years, when sexual organs and functions (such as menstruation) were considered dirty. It doesn't help that much of the street talk and profanity we hear chooses sexuality as its main subject. And yet our bodies are our vehicle for enjoying sex, and they are part of the gift that we give when we make love. It is hard to give ourselves over to the sexual experience when we feel that our body is ugly, inadequate or a vehicle of temptation and sin.

There are many ways we can move toward accepting and enjoying the body God has given us. We can get to know our body, take stock and discover what is beautiful, and accept those things that aren't quite what we'd wish. We can learn a simple appreciation of the many ways our body functions: "I really enjoy the things I can do in my body. I enjoy letting go and experiencing orgasm. I love a good game of softball or volleyball. I'm amazed that my body has given birth and nursed children. I'm so glad that I can comfort someone with a hug. Thank you, God, for this wonderful gift."

Being physically fit or at least physically active is a wonderful way of experiencing ourselves as a physical body. Walking, biking and participating in sports can heighten our feelings of gratitude for the gift of life in our bodies and keep us more in touch with our physical, sexual self. All of us—married or single—can embrace the "sexy" or sensual side of ourselves quite apart from the presence of a man in our life. One woman notices, "Swimming in warm water, dressing in silks, exercising until I feel 'high'—all of those things are sexual feelings to me. Even if I'm not involved with someone else, I can still feel sexually alive." Others are aware of their sexuality as an *energy,* and rather than being uncomfortable or ashamed of it, they channel it toward caring for those around them and making a difference in this world. We have many ways of learning to be at home in our body, and as we do so, we bring pleasure to the heart of God by enjoying the gift he has given.

Some women find that masturbation is another way of growing more comfortable with their bodies. Research indicates that although anywhere from 60 to 80 percent of women masturbate to orgasm, many women have strongly negative feelings about it. It's hard to know where all these negative feelings come from, but it's almost certain that some of our shame or fear about touching ourselves is formed very early in our development.

The Scriptures say nothing about this subject, and we now know that there are no harmful physical or medical effects from masturbating. Actually, there is ample evidence that the practice can be beneficial for married women. Women can learn a lot about their own sexual responses—which kinds of touch feel good and which are irritating, which body movements and positions enhance sexual response—from self-pleasuring. Too often women leave knowledge about their sexual anatomy to their husband or doctor because of their phobias about touching themselves, and they miss out on knowledge that would be helpful to their marital relationship.

Self-stimulation can also be very helpful for the married woman who has not yet learned to experience orgasm. For the woman who is uncomfortable with her body or with her body's sexual response, the freedom to explore in private may make it easier for her to share this knowledge with her husband and be responsive to him. A woman's comfort with and knowledge of her own body can greatly enhance the joint experience.

Unmarried adults often suffer in silence because there are two distinct schools of thought on singleness and masturbation. One belief is that the single person must be celibate in every sense of the word, avoiding sexual stimulation or experience of any kind. The other view sees sexuality as too much a part of the whole person to be completely repressed and ignored.

Christian writers and counselors fall into both camps. Some view the physical release of sexual tension as a gift from God for women who are single, helping them to embrace their sexuality. Masturbation is seen in some ways as a deterrent to sexual sin; some women have found that when they are feeling comfortable with and in control of their own sexuality, they are less likely to act inappropriately in their male-female friendships or to fall into sexual relationships out of desperation or the pressure of unmet sexual urges. Meanwhile, those who view masturbation as off limits maintain that there are nonsexual ways of channeling the sex drive, such as physical exercise, expression of creative gifts and service to others.

The most obvious negative about masturbation is its capability of controlling us. There are many things in this life that are good but have the potential to become enslaving (food, shopping, exercise) or to be used selfishly (sex, money, power). Any habit that causes us to reshape and reschedule the rest of our life has gained undue influence over us. In *The Gift of Sex,* Clifford and Joyce Penner offer three biblical guidelines by which we can evaluate whether masturbation has become a positive or negative activity in our lives. I have adapted them here:

1. *Is it loving?* If our behavior takes something away from our marriage partner, it is not loving. However, if masturbation helps alleviate pressure between two people who have differing degrees of sexual interest or helps a woman learn to be more responsive to her husband, then it could be viewed as a loving choice.

2. *Is it lustful?* Some people think that you have to lust in order to enjoy self-pleasuring. However, many people report that when they masturbate they think only of their spouse or the physical sensations they are experiencing.

3. *Is it addictive?* If a woman is masturbating excessively as a way of avoiding relationship issues or emotional needs, this is not healthy. If a woman uses masturbation as a way of becoming more comfortable with her body and her sexuality, it can be life-enhancing.

Whichever view you take, if you are single, it is most important that you think through the reasons for your decision to allow yourself this practice or to prohibit it. We are in the most danger of making poor sexual choices when we neglect to take an honest, well-reasoned look at it. This area, as much as any other, should be explored in the context of prayer. God, who created us as sexual beings, longs to be with us and give us wisdom in this important are of our lives.

Women who are experiencing sexual fulfillment know not to use sex as a weapon. Because of the way relationships between men and women have traditionally been structured (with the man being dominant and the woman being his supporter), it can be quite natural for a woman to see sex as her only weapon in a situation where she feels she has very little power.

In the workplace, a woman may be sorely tempted to flirt with the boss just a little, feeling that this is the only way for her to get into his good graces. In marriage it doesn't take long for a wife to figure out that withholding what her husband wants most puts her in a powerful position; she may begin to see this as her only way of registering a complaint or displeasure. The fact that these tactics often get results makes it easy to fall into a pattern of using sex or withholding it—without even being aware of what we are doing. The resulting sexual difficulties are not really about sex but are indicators of other problems in the relationship, such as an imbalance of power or an inability to resolve conflict.

Ann Birk, director of a sex therapy program in Boston, says that the major predictor of sexual dysfunction in women is chronic and underexpressed anger. When a woman is angry with her husband or boyfriend and that anger cannot vent itself, it can have a direct and crippling effect on sexuality. In most cases, repressed anger and loving abandon just can't exist side by side. Birk recalls the case of one young woman who was very angry with her husband because he was rarely home. "She could not bring herself to confront him with her anger and developed a vaginal condition that prevented her from having intercourse. As soon as she was able to confront him, to say, 'I need you home more,' the condition vanished almost immediately and she was able to function sexually."

I do not want to make this process seem simpler than it is. It takes hard work to resolve these issues to the satisfaction of both parties in a relationship. However, many women have found that when they learn to deal more directly and effectively with anger and other relationship issues, they begin to flourish sexually.

Women who are experiencing sexual satisfaction know they have to conserve time and energy for it. One of the biggest reasons married couples do not have sex is their pace of life. After the job, children, school functions, meals and care of the home, couples end up in bed very tired. And when you're not getting enough sleep, it's easy to let sex go by the wayside or to have it but not put too much into it.

Good sex takes energy. The sexually vital woman knows this and makes a conscious effort not to use up her last bit of energy at night washing the floor, putting last-minute touches on a presentation or talking on the phone to a friend. There certainly are crunch times when it is inevitable that we fall into bed exhausted or don't even make it to bed at the same time. But the woman who is enjoying a fulfilling sex life does not allow this to become a pattern. She lets the floor go, gets up a little earlier in the morning or gracefully excuses herself from the lengthy phone conversation. She doesn't see sex as being just for her husband; she understands that she needs it too. The warmth of being close, the release of tension, the reawakening of loving feelings that get lost in the rush of everyday tasks and schedules are blessings that she cannot afford to lose. And so, with at least some regularity, she saves part of herself for it.

THE JOY OF SEX

Psychiatrist M. Scott Peck tells of working for many months with a "rigid, frigid woman in her mid-thirties" who underwent a sudden and profound Christian conversion and within three weeks became orgasmic for the first time in her life. Peck concluded that when this woman was able to give herself wholeheartedly to God, in very short order she was able to give herself wholeheartedly to a human partner. He quotes these words of a friend: "The sexual and spiritual parts of ourselves lie so close together that it is hardly possible to arouse one without the other."

The Bible tells us that our body is a "temple of the Holy Spirit" (1 Corinthians 6:19). In some unexplainable way, God's Spirit indwells us, making our body a place where we can meet and know him. Since sexuality is such an important aspect of our bodily self, it too can become a means of encountering God. All parts of the human experience are somehow connected. All aspects of our humanity, including our sexuality, are spiritual and hold the possibility for abundant living, for the experience of grace and for the imprint of the divine. The Reverend Alice Peterson, pastor and spiritual director, notes, "Many think that sexuality will go away or at least become quiescent as we grow spiritually. On the contrary! As we abide more closely to the God who is the source of all creative energy, the God of the incarnation, we begin to experience sexual energy in a new way, as a holy, inalienable, generative force."

ALL PARTS OF THE HUMAN EXPERIENCE ARE SOMEHOW CONNECTED. ALL ASPECTS OF OUR HUMANITY, INCLUDING OUR SEXUALITY, ARE SPIRITUAL AND HOLD THE POSSIBILITY FOR ABUNDANT LIVING, FOR THE EXPERIENCE OF GRACE AND FOR THE IMPRINT OF THE DIVINE.

Our delight in living in our body, our joy in physical expressions of love that are appropriate to the relationships God has given us, the capacity for communion that keeps us seeking meaningful connection with others—all of these are ways of bringing glory to the Giver of the gift of our sexuality. They are a powerful testimony to the fullness that comes when we live in harmony with him.

SPIRITUAL EXERCISES

Alone with God

Silence. As you come to the end of this chapter, take a few moments to sit with God in the silence of your heart. You might want to reflect on one or more of these questions:

- How do you feel about the sexual, womanly part of yourself?
- Does it feel like a gift or a burden, a place of gladness or a place of shame?
- What are the life experiences that seem to shape your perspective?

Prayer and journaling. Review what you have just read, noticing the places of resonance and resistance that you have highlighted. Few of us have had the opportunity to reflect on our sexuality as a part of God's call to spiritual transformation.

- Where in this chapter did you identify (or not) with other women's experiences?
- What was your response to the idea that the sexual part of ourselves and the spiritual part of ourselves are connected?
- What difference would it make in the way you express yourself sexually if you really knew that to be true?
- Which of the stereotypes do you need to let go of in order to experience your sexuality more freely as a gift from God?
- Do you sense God calling you to a deeper place of healing for any harmful sexual influences that were imposed on you?

Allow yourself time to journal about your questions and desires in this area. Tell God what's true about you right now and what you long for. Then listen for his response.

Invitations. God, are you inviting me to respond to what I have read today? In what way?

Experiencing the
Transformations of Motherhood

Of course a mother gives up a lot for her child: blood, sleep, tears, not to mention time, money, and peace of mind. But a mother must not feel obliged to give up herself. Not unless she wants to raise a motherless child.

LISA CRONIN WOHL

It is difficult to admit how hard mothering has been for me. It's not the mechanics of it—the pregnancy, the birthing, knowing what to feed when, figuring out what to do when they're sick. No, what I've struggled with most is the relentlessness of the demands, the never-ending nature of the needs to which I must attend, the interruptions, the constantly delayed gratification of my own desires, the uncertainty about how my children will turn out after all the parental words of wisdom have been said and all the hard work has been done.

I know I am not alone in my ambivalence. One friend mused, "I think a lot of women struggle with their role as mother. For me, mothering is nothing like I thought it would be. . . . I always pictured myself spending hours reading to my daughter, but I don't. She wants me to get down on the floor and play with her, but I've discovered that I just don't like to play. . . . My self-concept has really suffered because I haven't lost the weight I put on during pregnancy. I hardly ever have reason to get dressed up, and nobody listens to me as though I have anything intelligent to say like they did when I was working."

A STRUGGLE WITHIN A STRUGGLE

The fact that we find mothering more difficult than we had imagined is a truth of the female experience that can be hard to talk about. Society's expectations of us and our own expectations of ourselves are so different from our actual experience of things. Media and child-care experts present images of motherhood that can be hard to live up to. We are supposed to be utterly devoted to our children, always ready to care for them and to do housework. We're not supposed to feel anything but love for our children.

Culturally and religiously, motherhood has been emphasized as a woman's highest calling much more insistently than fatherhood has been for men. We hear the biblical message that children are a gift from God, but when our experience doesn't match our belief system, we're not quite sure what to do with ourselves. How-to books and magazine articles written by earth-mother types who have an unlimited supply of ideas for planning day trips, craft projects, holiday traditions and morning devotionals rarely encourage us. They just further overwhelm us with an unattainable ideal.

The struggle that women experience on an individual level takes place in a society that is grappling with the issue of "what to do with the children." A quick glance at magazine and newspaper headlines over the last decades reveals a powerful picture that requires little commentary: "Are We Forgetting the Kids?" "After School Orphans," "Who's Minding America's Children?" and "Forever Theirs: The Dark

Side of the Job from Which You Cannot Resign." (This last one was accompanied by a large drawing of a mother gagged and bound to a chair, held captive by a child with a gun!)

We have been told that we can have it all—a good marriage, children, a successful career, material possessions and other personal achievements—and that children don't have to interfere with any of these pursuits. At best, children are often viewed as an option that we can fit in at our convenience or decide against altogether; at worst, they are seen as a nuisance or an interruption. At the same time, we worry about how we're doing at caring for our children. Are they watching too much TV? getting too little discipline? eating too much junk food?

After reading the litany of threats facing our children today— drive-by shootings, illegal drugs, sexual molesters and kidnappers, murderers and rapists taking children from their own bedrooms, degrading television programming, and commercials featuring dancing condoms—it is easy to feel overwhelmed by the responsibilities of parenting, the majority of which still fall to women in our society. The fact that our culture no longer supports basic morality and religious truth as it has in the past just adds to the gravity of the situation. We Christians labor under the weighty realization that, to a certain extent, the future of our children depends on our ability to counter the culture in which they live and breathe. How do we experience truth and freedom in the midst of such pressure?

THE PARADOX OF MOTHERHOOD

Throughout my years of parenting I have struggled, questioned, argued and cried. Yet in the midst of God's call to mothering I am being transformed as I trust in God's sovereignty and receive the blessings he bestows through my children.

In the early years of parenting, a kind of awe develops as we realize that *this* child—our child—is given to us and to this world for a purpose that God himself knows and intends to make known in his time. It's not only that children in general are a blessing but that the specific children God sends to us are given as his blessing for our lives. Some of these blessings are fleeting in nature: the pleasure of soft baby cheeks perfect for nuzzling and pug noses perfect for kissing, the pride that fills our heart as we watch a child—our child—run with strength and grace down a soccer field, the fullness that we feel as we don pajamas and cuddle under blankets to watch a movie together on a snowy night, the amazement of seeing strengths surface in our child that are quite different from our own.

Moments of blessedness come when we are least expecting them. They are the moments of joy that give us perspective when the stress and tedium of childrearing threaten to overwhelm us. Sometimes these moments are gone as quickly as they come, but we can hold them in our hearts as evidence that God sent these children to bless us in ways we hadn't imagined.

Other blessings are of the long-lasting sort, blessings we carry with us into eternity. The greatest of these is the blessedness of knowing that we have influenced another soul to embrace Christ as Savior; this is the one treasure that you *can* "take with you." When Chris and I sent our oldest daughter, Charity, off to college, it was hard for me to express the gratitude and awe, the deep love and satisfaction, that I felt about sending this daughter into the world—one who is strong and beautiful and clear about who she is in God, willing and ready to do her part in turning her world upside down for Christ. As I expressed in a letter written on her eighteenth birthday, "You are becoming yourself in ways that some women take all their lives to achieve. (Some never do!) I truly cannot figure out where you came from! I see glimpses of myself in you, but you are also much *more* than what I am and I am reminded that you came from God."

MOTHERING HAS PROVIDED YET ANOTHER CONTEXT
FOR MY OWN TRANSFORMATION.

So it is quite a paradox to find that an area where I have struggled so deeply has become one of my deepest sources of joy and pride. I am aware of deep satisfaction as my daughters emerge into such true expressions of the persons God created them to be. I am also aware that mothering has provided yet another context for my own transformation. It has required me to confront levels of selfishness and pride that might have been left unchallenged were it not for the opportunities that mothering presents. The experience of being a mother has called me to new levels of faith and perseverance that might have otherwise gone unexplored. Seeing my character deficiencies surface as I relate to my children and listening to my daughters' unedited evaluation of my Christianity as it is lived out before them have provided me with wonderful growth—when I have been able to remain open!

These are the blessings God intends for us when he gives us the gift of children. In a culture where it seems that children are God's least-wanted blessing, it is the eye of faith that knows how to see them and the believing heart that knows how to receive them.

GOD'S INVITATION TO LOVE CHILDREN

Hannah's is a true parenting success story. Perhaps you remember the story of this woman who struggled with infertility and promised God that if he gave her a son she would dedicate him to the Lord's service (see 1 Samuel 1 and 2). The Lord answered her prayer and gave her a son, whom she named Samuel. When Samuel was weaned, Hannah kept her promise and took Samuel to the temple in Shiloh to serve God with the priest Eli. Hannah's early training stood Samuel in good stead, and despite Eli's spiritual deadness and some poor influences (Eli's unruly sons), Samuel went on to become one of the greatest prophets, priests and judges Israel ever knew.

Although the details of Samuel's upbringing are a bit unusual, the story of Hannah and her son reminds us that God can work in a variety of situations to produce children who will serve him faithfully throughout their lives. This is of particular comfort to single parents who must try to fill the roles of mother and father while trying to generate all or most of the family income. When a situation seems impossible, Hannah's story reminds us that God can be trusted to bring our children through whatever the disadvantages of our situation happen to be. Hannah's story also underscores basic elements of effective parenting and leads us to ask ourselves if we are willing to love our children in some very practical ways.

Love them enough to welcome them. Sometimes in the throes of mothering we forget that children are human beings created and known by God. Hannah knew even before her child was born that God was involved in the life that formed in her. Psalm 139 indicates that God knows and forms each child in the womb. Before they are born, God already has a plan for them. As he pointed out to Jeremiah: "Before I formed you in the womb I knew you, and before you were born I consecrated you; I appointed you a prophet to the nations" (1:5). Men and women of the Bible were highly aware of the fact that life does not begin merely because of human action—God is always involved in conception and birth. Eve said, "I have gotten a manchild with the help of the Lord" (Genesis 4:1 NASB), the Lord was the one who opened Leah's womb (Genesis 29:31), and Ruth 4:13 says, "The LORD enabled her [Ruth] to conceive, and she gave birth to a son" (NASB). Recognizing that God is the source of our children's lives is foundational to understanding the magnitude and the privilege of the call to parent.

Believing that children are a blessing, Hannah prayed that God would give her this gift and welcomed her son when he was born. Her response mirrored Christ's welcoming attitude toward children in Matthew 19. Even though the disciples were anxious to shoo them away, Christ used them as an example of faith and said that when we welcome children, we welcome him.

As women, we have a unique opportunity to welcome little ones by bearing them in our bodies. This is the first sacrifice we make, and it is a sacrifice! In a body-worshiping culture such as ours, it is no small thing to realize that your breasts and belly may never be the same! But that is only the beginning. In her book *Sacred Dwelling: A Spirituality of Family Life,* Wendy Wright speaks about what this welcoming really means:

> To welcome a child is to accept responsibility for another person twenty-four hours a day, seven days a week, for a good many years. Ultimately, it is to welcome the unfolding mystery of an entire lifetime's joys and pains as your own. To welcome a child is to give priority to the unpredictability of another life, to tend to it in sickness, no matter what you had otherwise planned, to allow your plans and dreams to be altered, even set aside, because of another's need. To welcome a child is to learn to think and speak in response to a different and constantly changing worldview, to be outside of your own frame of reference. You learn patience and judgment and are confronted with

your own very real and heretofore untested limitations. To welcome a child is to recognize the surprising expansiveness of your own capacity to love and to confront the shattering truth of your own violence and self-centeredness. To welcome a child is to have your heart stretched, made capable of loving in a new and unrepeatable way.

God calls fathers and mothers to welcome children into their lives, making a place where their emotional, spiritual and physical needs are met.

Love them enough to make them a priority. Hannah was forced by her unusual circumstances to see her time with Samuel as a very brief window of opportunity for training and loving, and she took full advantage of it. In Jewish culture, weaning (which literally means "dealt fully with") was accomplished when a child was around three years old. Until Hannah felt that she had dealt fully with her son, she didn't even take the annual trip to Shiloh to worship at the temple. She knew that the time would come when it would be right for her to go and fulfill her promise. But until the Lord freed her to do that, she made Samuel her priority.

Although our window of opportunity may not be as small as it was for Hannah and Samuel, it is relatively short in the whole scheme of things. In the early years especially, most children want to be with their parents more than anyone else and are wide open to our influence. What a privilege this is! It's not long before children reach the developmental stage in which they are embarrassed to be seen with parents and want to hang out with their friends rather than their family. What could possibly be worth giving up being with my children when they want to be with me more than anyone else in the world?

Love them enough to discipline them. The story of Samuel (1 Samuel 1–4) offers a poignant study in contrasts. While Samuel ministered to the Lord and experienced his presence, Eli's sons grew up to be scoundrels. The Bible says that they had no regard for the Lord or for the duties of a priest to the people. They stole from the offerings people brought and seduced the women who served at the place of worship. Eli knew about his sons' sinful behavior but only offered weak reprimands. Finally God intervened and said to Eli, "I chose your family out of all the families in Israel to perform the sacred duties of priests. I revealed myself in a special way to your ancestors. Why then have you honored your sons more than me by fattening yourselves on the choicest parts of every offering of my people Israel?" (1 Samuel 2:27-29, my paraphrase).

To Samuel, God communicated this message: "I am about to punish Eli's house forever, for the iniquity that he knew, because his sons were blaspheming God, and he did not restrain them" (1 Samuel 3:13, my paraphrase). And that is exactly what happened. It wasn't long before Hophni and Phinehas were killed in battle. When Eli heard the news he fell from his seat, broke his neck and died. Tragic endings to tragic lives.

The point is that we don't do anyone any favors by refusing to discipline our children. In fact, we do our children, ourselves and our society a great disservice when we allow them to be disrespectful, immoral and undisciplined. We have the same problem today that Eli had, although perhaps for our own set of reasons.

Children have an uncanny ability to play on the guilt feelings to which today's parents are so susceptible. When I am stressed out because I have taken on too much and I'm not sure if the kids are getting what they need, it is very easy to give in when they accuse us of being unfair in requiring them to pull their weight around the house, behave respectfully, or live without something they want. Then, in an effort to assuage my guilt, I tend to spend the time when I am available overcompensating. However, when I am more consistently available for my children's legitimate needs, I am much more confident about insisting that they do the dishes, accept the fact that they cannot have another sleepover, or respond respectfully to the limits we have set in our home. When I know they are getting what they really need from us—time, attention, limits, physical needs (not necessarily wants) met—then I am a lot less likely to give in to doubt when it comes time for strong discipline or saying no.

Limits set by loving parents are good for children, because young people who do not know how to work, how to respect authority and how to control themselves will not get very far in life. In fact, these qualities are becoming so rare that just by cultivating them, our children will distinguish themselves and be well on their way to success in work, marriage, family life and spiritual service. We cannot expect them to have this long-range perspective while they are young; that's why we must keep it for them until they are old enough to realize how important it is.

Love them enough to share our spiritual journey. We do not know for sure how many years Hannah was able to spend with Samuel before she took him to the temple. However, we do know that in whatever time she had, she trained him effectively and cultivated his spiritual life. Even though he was surrounded by poor influences at the temple, Samuel continued to serve the Lord faithfully. And even though Eli was ineffective as a father and as a spiritual leader ("the word of the LORD was rare in those days; visions were not widespread," 1 Samuel 3:1), Samuel began to hear and respond to God's voice. In fact, "as Samuel grew up, the LORD was with him and let none of his words fall to the ground. And all Israel . . . knew that Samuel was a trustworthy prophet of the LORD. . . . For the LORD revealed himself to Samuel at Shiloh . . . and the word of Samuel came to all Israel" (1 Samuel 3:19—4:1).

The amazing truth here is that God had given up trying to communicate with the elderly priest Eli and chose to communicate with this young boy who had a heart that was sensitized to the voice of God. It was through this mere child that the horror of spiritual drought in the land of Israel was relieved. Where do you think Samuel's strong character and spiritual receptivity came from? My guess is that it was a combination of the heart God gave him and the training he received in his home.

Just think! Our children also have the potential to be those through whom God speaks and from whom a river of life can flow to those who thirst for a taste of God's presence. But raising up the kind of children who will know God and bless others doesn't happen by accident. It happens in homes where children are important, where limits are set and where spiritual awareness is cultivated.

Another observation comes from Deuteronomy 6:6-9: effective child training is a mixture of structured and spontaneous instruction. These verses presuppose that both parents are with their children enough to be able to teach them throughout the day as they walk and talk together and as they drop off to sleep and wake. These informal times of training and instilling values are just as important as more structured family prayers and Bible reading.

As children grow older, it can also be appropriate to open up those places where we are still in process—wrestling with unanswered questions and the unfinished places in our soul. During the time when I was questioning my long-held beliefs about God's view of women, I did not know where the questions would take me spiritually or how they would affect my relationships. As my struggle deepened, it became impossible to hide my emerging emotions from those closest to me—including my three daughters. As much as I might have wished that I could have traveled this part of my journey in seclusion, that was not my situation. I had three little girls watching their mother fight for her spiritual life.

At one point in particular, when I needed to drop out of church for a while in order to let old wounds heal, I remember crying out to God with questions about how this would affect my girls' spiritual development. How would they possibly understand the fact that their dad took them to church while their mom stayed home? What meanings would they give to this later on?

Eventually I realized that I needed to take what seemed like a huge step of faith as a mother. I had to believe and trust that if I stayed faithful to the way in which God was calling me to go deeper with him, healing the pains of the past and forming something new for the future, then something good would be in that for my daughters. Perhaps letting them in on my own struggle would give them more freedom to wrestle with God when they needed to, and to ultimately find that "One can never wrestle enough with God if one does so out of pure regard for truth. Christ likes us to prefer truth to him, because before being Christ, he is truth. If one turns aside from him to go toward the truth, one will not go far before falling into his arms." Thus, in age-appropriate ways, I began to be more intentional about sharing this portion of my faith journey with our daughters, letting them see my struggle and hear my questions. I began trusting in God's care for them, trusting that they could benefit from knowing the truth of my experience and its impact on our family. And I have no regrets.

Today, as I witness their emerging strength and clarity about who they are as young women, I know these things have something to do with parts of my journey they have witnessed. I am convinced that the best thing we as mothers have to give our children is our own transforming selves. Whatever we leave unresolved within ourselves—due to fear or laziness or lack of initiative—will be passed on to them as unresolved issues. On the other hand, opening up to God's transforming work in our lives can become one of the greatest treasures we could ever offer.

Love them enough to let them go. As we dropped Charity off at college a few years ago, I couldn't help but remember her first day of kindergarten. I had walked to pick her up, and as we walked home, she insisted on walking a couple of blocks ahead. I called her back and tried to convince her to walk and talk with me, but she said, "Can we do that when we get home? I want to be a big girl." There was no malice. No impertinence. Just the honest expression of a little girl trying to grow up.

So we walked that way, and I had the pleasure of watching her walk ahead of me—ponytail bobbing, backpack carried proudly. Every block or so she would turn around and wave, just making sure I was there. And I would wave back, trying to communicate with every wave that I loved her and was proud of her and that it was okay that she wanted to walk alone. It was a picture of the process parents and children begin at birth: the process of letting go, of allowing our children to gain their independence little by little. It is, after all, what we raise them for, and we must never forget it.

For Hannah, the moment of letting go all the way came much sooner than it does for most of us. After weaning Samuel, she took him back to the temple to dedicate him to the Lord's work, just as she had promised. It is hard to imagine that she was unaware of Eli's lack of spiritual effectiveness or Hophni and Phinehas's sinful behavior. Yet the time had come for her to trust that the training she had done and Samuel's own relationship with God would give him the moorings he needed. Certainly that is what we must trust as we face those moments when we must say goodbye.

Fortunately, letting go comes gradually for most of us, one goodbye preparing us for the next. The first time we leave our baby with Grandma prepares us for the church nursery. The first day of school prepares us for that first overnight. Dropping them off at the big junior high or high school prepares us for the day we drop them off at college. Teaching them to choose their dates wisely and then letting them go prepares us to let them go with the one they choose to marry. Dedicating our children to the Lord at birth, as Hannah did, helps prepare us for the day when he calls them into service that may take them far from us.

We seek to achieve a balance between letting our children go in age-appropriate ways and providing the undergirding for their explorations. We must not hold them too tightly, yet we must always be there in the background, waving at them with support and love, ready to come to their aid when they need us, protecting them from dangers they are not quite ready to handle. And somewhere along the way, as we negotiate their transition into adulthood, we become more than parents and children. We become friends.

GIVING TO OUR CHILDREN WITHOUT LOSING OURSELVES

I have experienced a wide range of thoughts and feelings about my role as mother. I have spent time thinking that the grass looks greener on the side of the fence where women carry briefcases and dress in something besides jeans. In fact, I have been back and forth over that fence several times. I have also taken a long hard look at the inequities women have experienced as a result of having so much of the responsibility for homemaking and parenting placed on them. I have had days when anger and frustration have threatened to overwhelm me. And in the midst of all that, I have come to realize that there is no other area in my life in which the ramifications of my choices are so far reaching and the potential for regret so great.

While motherhood is a privilege that offers great joys and great challenges, we have to remain clear about the fact that it is one part of a whole life lived for kingdom purposes. Just as it is a grave mistake to invest our relationships with men with the weight of our need for self-esteem, identity and purpose, it is also a mistake to invest our mothering with all our hopes and dreams for meaning in this life. While motherhood is a deeply rewarding experience to which God calls most women, motherhood is only half a life's work.

Thirty-five is the age at which most women send their last child off to school, leaving many years for them to make other meaningful contributions to the kingdom of God here on earth. Many who have not kept their mothering in perspective with the greater call of God on their life find themselves feeling useless after their children leave the nest, and they have very little sense of what they should do next. They may end up biding time in dead-end jobs that do not capitalize on their giftedness or do not give them a sense that they are contributing to a cause that really matters. The sense of not knowing who they are apart from their role as a mother can be overwhelming when they begin to realize it.

Sometimes it seems like all these issues together create a Catch-22 situation that is impossible to find our way out of. We fear that the truths we want to embrace will conflict with the realities of daily life and the commitments that we care about. During such times when it feels like these realities are completely conflicting, all I can do is carry my questions into God's presence over and over again. I do this because I trust him. I do this because I know that he cares equally about me and about my children; he alone can give me perspective and help me put my life and the lives of my children together in a way that is best for all of us in the long run. I need his help to find the middle road that women must walk, a road that runs between two harmful extremes—neglecting our children and neglecting ourselves.

The only way to find the middle road and stay on it is to keep looking to God for guidance as each choice presents itself. I cling to his promise in Psalm 32: "I will instruct you . . . in the way which you should go; I will counsel you with my Eye upon you" (verse 8 NASB). With his loving eyes on me and my eyes on him, I have gotten better at knowing, "Yes, this ministry will fit right now . . . No, this class will take too much of my energy . . . Two evenings out this week, not three . . . No committee work now, but maybe after this project is finished . . . Time to put my own reading away and read to the children . . . The kids have gotten what they need from me today, now I can give some time to other work . . . Oops, I overdid it today; I'll do some adjusting tomorrow." God has been faithful to lead me into new ways of balancing and embracing the particular dimensions of my gifts and family callings.

As I have continued to bring my wrestling to God and open my heart to what he wants to teach me about being a mother, I've noticed that some concerns pale into insignificance while other concerns give birth to certainty. One truth I have become more certain of is that *children in our culture are in danger.* And that danger is not just "out there" in the big bad world. Our children are also in danger because, as a generation, they have suffered our neglect, our indifference and our inability to do what it takes to keep our families together.

Recent studies show that during unsupervised hours, latchkey children of all social and economic groups are twice as likely to abuse drugs, engage in sexual intercourse (one psychologist mentions that usually a girl has her first sexual experience in her or her boyfriend's empty house), join gangs or contribute to juvenile violent crime. These children may be extraordinarily isolated and lose out on valuable life-shaping experiences with friends and role models during the critical period of adolescent development.

I CONSIDER MYSELF TO BE A LIBERATED WOMAN. BUT THERE IS NO WAY I CAN, NOR WOULD I WANT TO, "LIBERATE" MYSELF FROM THE FACT THAT I HAVE CHILDREN AND THEY NEED ME.

The message of these facts is simple: our children need us! I consider myself to be a liberated woman. But there is no way I can, nor would I want to, "liberate" myself from the fact that I have children and they need me.

The answer to the question of what to do with children is not for women to pull out and renege on our God-given responsibility. The answer is for men and women together to fall on our faces before God and confess selfishness and upside-down values where they exist. To believe that children are a blessing and to translate that belief into making them a priority in our lives. To slow down our frantic rush for success, money and power so that we can adequately supervise our children all the way through their teenage years. To share parenting responsibilities so that women and men alike can nurture other parts of themselves even as they nurture children. To cast ourselves on God for wisdom and strength. To daily inquire of God, "What will it require of me to nurture the emotional, physical and spiritual well-being of my children? How do you want to transform me in the process?"

ACCEPTING THE RESPONSIBILITY

As mothers, we are called to rest in the sovereignty of God in giving us children but also to accept responsibility to make informed choices. Bill Hybels wisely encourages newly married couples not to make the choice to have children unadvisedly. He mentions several important considerations that should inform such a decision. "First," he says, "newly married couples should devote themselves to solidifying their marriage before they even consider having children. Raising a healthy, well-adjusted, Christ-honoring child in today's world almost demands a strong marriage and family unit." He also recommends that couples consider whether either of them carries "the deep trauma of a painful or tragic past" that they have not yet worked through fully. Considering the implications of passing on their wounds to another generation, they should make the investment in dealing with unresolved issues before bringing a child into such a complicated scene. (These issues might be substance abuse, sexual abuse, domestic violence, parents who were unable to give love, or other similar struggles and traumas.) The fact of the matter is that "it takes time and energy to raise children. Young couples hoping to find a system of child rearing that doesn't inconvenience them or overload their already full schedules should rethink their decision. It may be they're missing the whole point of having children."

A couple may also decide, after listening to God and paying careful attention to what he is doing in their lives, not to have children in order to participate in building Christ's kingdom by pursuing full-time careers in ministry or in the marketplace. It is unfortunate that in some Christian circles couples who choose not to have children are considered incomplete, selfish or unfaithful to the whole idea of marriage. Yet we can't ignore the "normal" families that have turned out to be quite unhealthy because someone didn't count the cost—either to the children or the parents—of adding family members to a life already consumed in ministry and career.

IS THIS A JOB FOR SUPERMOM?

I am convinced that one of the reasons women today struggle so greatly with our role as mothers is that the weight of responsibility of nurturing and rearing children tends to fall primarily on us. God's instruction for us to attend to our children is huge and multifaceted, but when men and women are committed to it together, it is much less overwhelming.

I do not need another book on how to be a better mother. I do not need a support group. What I have needed is my husband, the father of my children, to participate more fully with me in this great call of God on our lives. I have needed to hear him say with words and with actions, "You are not alone. These children are just as much my responsibility as they are yours. Together we have received the high call of parenting."

Just as the men and women of Israel together received detailed instruction for caring for children (Deuteronomy 6:6-9), so I have needed to know and experience in relationship with my husband, Chris, that raising children is not "women's work" but kingdom work that is worthy of the very best we both have to offer. And it has been in working together—rather than in listening to one more sermon or reading one more book—that my feelings of being overwhelmed and isolated and inadequate have begun to subside. I have often said that there is nothing more attractive than a man who helps. In this case, there is nothing more attractive than a man who considers himself to be a partner in the responsibilities and privilege of parenting—not only in word but also in deed. It is one of God's greatest gifts!

Nurturing children, generating income and following God's call to minister to a lost world can be blended into a rich family life in a multitude of ways. It should not necessarily be assumed that the wife's ministry or career is the one that must come to a grinding halt. In some cases it is feasible for the husband, the wife or both to slow down, adjust and find ways to give and take in order to accommodate the arrival of children.

One couple I know (both pastors now) has made a variety of arrangements throughout the life of their family. Steve finished his graduate work B.C. (before children), but Jamie had not finished hers when they had their first child. During the early months of his son's life, Steve worked part time and helped out with childcare while Jamie finished her degree. Then for four years, Steve worked in his career of choice while Jamie stayed home with child number one and added another. At a previously arranged time they switched, and Steve stayed at home for three years while Jamie got her career off the ground.

Today the children are well on their way to adulthood, and both Jamie and Steve are settled into their respective pastorates. Steve looks back on the years he stayed home with his children as "the best years of my life" and says, "I know that I did something that was right for my children, my wife and even me." He concludes,

> More and more fathers are investing themselves in parenting because they realize there is joy and satisfaction there that can be found nowhere else. And they realize that their children need them in ways that are important and unique. . . . Who better than a father to mold healthy self-image through play and everyday activities like these [playing horsey on the living-room floor]? Who better than a father to teach his children that they are important and worthwhile by investing his time and energy

into them? . . . Fathers who stay at home with their children have the same goal as everyone else—to bring up happy, well-adjusted children. When parenting is shared, [this] objective may be more easily attained.

The privilege of parenting with another person is a God-given gift. Each family needs to find its own way through it. When women and men share the responsibility of providing for the physical, spiritual and emotional well-being of their children, neither has to be weighted down with burdens heavier than God intended for them to bear alone. Together we can open ourselves to the transformation God invites us to through the blessings and the wonders of our children.

SPIRITUAL EXERCISES

Alone with God

Silence. As you come to the end of this chapter, take a few moments to sit with God in the silence of your heart and allow yourself to experience the full range of your feelings and thoughts about being a mother at this particular stage. Don't judge yourself at all. Let yourself feel the joy and privilege, the frustration and pain, the longing and the satisfaction, the things that you're sure of and the things you're questioning.

Prayer and journaling. Review what you have just read, noticing the places of resonance and resistance that you have highlighted. Allow yourself time to reflect on and journal about your experiences and longings as a woman who is also a mother. Tell God what's true about you right now and what you long for. Then listen for his response.

- Where were places in the reading that touched areas of deep concern in you?

- What places sparked joy?
- What was your heart's response to some of the research that was presented along with the biblical truth?
- Where did God seem to be touching a place of desire and commitment in you?
- What opportunities for transformation are being given to you now in the midst of your mothering?

Invitations. God, how are you inviting me to respond to what I've read today?

Finding God in the Midst of Difficulty

Be patient towards all that is unsolved in your heart and try to love the
questions themselves. . . . Do not now seek the answers, which cannot be
given you because you would not be able to live them. Live the questions now.
Perhaps you will then gradually, without noticing it, live along some
distant day into the answer.

RANIER MARIA RILKE, *LETTERS TO A YOUNG POET*

Every now and then I enjoy window shopping in jewelry stores. I am always amazed at how the cut stones, especially the diamonds, shine so brilliantly. Even the cheapest, most ordinary diamonds look beautiful under the bright lights when displayed against a background of black velvet.

It can be that way with people, too. Sometimes, against the backdrop of pain, tragedy or difficulty, a beauty shines forth that is accentuated by the darkness of the surrounding circumstances. Abigail was such a woman—a diamond whose beauty and worth shone against the backdrop of a difficult, heartbreaking marriage. Abigail was everything we would like to be—godly, intelligent and beautiful. However, the most striking thing about her is that she managed to

live a godly life in what, for most of us, would have been an intolerable situation.

STRONG UNDER PRESSURE

Abigail's story is found in 1 Samuel 25. The writer described her as
"intelligent and beautiful in appearance," while her husband, Nabal,
was "harsh and evil in his dealings" (25:3 NASB). As the story unfolds,
we see more evidence that Nabal was no knight in shining armor: He
was impossible to reason with, he was selfish and rude, and he was
an alcoholic who became abusive when he was drunk.

It is not hard to imagine the disappointment and loneliness Abigail
lived with on a daily basis. Certainly she had some of the same hopes
that we all do for love and companionship in marriage. How she
must have wished that her life were different; perhaps at times she
cried out to God to deliver her from the pain of such a hurtful, unhealthy relationship.

One day, the normal stress of living with a difficult man escalated
into a true crisis. David, who was running from a jealous King Saul,
happened to be hiding out in the desert of Paran, which bordered
Nabal's property. During that time, David and the six hundred men
who were with him provided protection for Nabal's shepherds while
they were in the fields. At one point David politely requested payment for services rendered, and Nabal responded with rudeness and
ingratitude, denying any knowledge at all of David or the protection
his men had provided. This sent David into a murderous rage, and
he quickly organized four hundred of his men to kill all the males in
Nabal's household (verses 13, 21-22).

One of Nabal's servants understood the gravity of the situation but
also understood that Nabal was "so ill-natured that no one can speak
to him" (verse 17). So he went straight to Abigail and explained the

situation. She obviously had the complete confidence of her household staff, and with good reason. She immediately swung into action, initiating a plan that was characterized by insight, godly wisdom, courage and diplomacy. Her direct and insightful intervention with David (verses 18, 25-38) quickly defused this volatile situation.

David, this great man of God, was impressed by Abigail's discernment, and he listened and responded to the wisdom of her words. He realized that what she was saying was true. If he did act out of uncontrolled anger as he had planned, he would shed innocent blood rather than leaving vengeance up to God. At best, this would place a permanent blot on his character; at worst, it could disqualify him as a leader for the people of Israel. So he blessed her, received the provisions she had brought and turned away from his murderous intent.

Abigail must have been very relieved at the outcome of her peace-keeping mission, but when she got home, she faced another problem. Nabal had been partying and he was drunk; it was not a good time to tell him about the disaster they had so narrowly escaped (verse 36). She wisely waited until the next morning to fill him in, and when he heard it, "his heart died within him; he became like a stone" (verse 37). Apparently paralyzed by a stroke, he died ten days later. When David heard about what had become of Nabal, he was thankful that he had waited and allowed God to avenge his cause. He also sent a proposal of marriage to Abigail, and she accepted in what appears to have been a very happy ending.

FROM DIFFICULTIES TO DIAMONDS

Despite the fact that Abigail's marriage was probably arranged, as was the custom of the day, her situation is all too contemporary. Even women who have had the opportunity to choose their marriage partner often end up with unexpected difficulties. One author, saying

Abigail would be a perfect candidate for an Al-Anon recovery group or a support group for "women who love too much," cites her rush from an abusive marriage into a polygamous one as a foolish choice.

But there was more to Abigail than that. She was not living in denial, and she didn't shy away from a realistic assessment of her situation: "My lord, do not take seriously this ill-natured fellow, Nabal, for as his name is, so is he; Nabal is his name, and folly is with him" (verse 25). She had excellent management and interpersonal skills, as evidenced by the way she handled conflict and related with the household staff. She worked effectively for peace by clarifying the issues in a nonthreatening way and showed tremendous spiritual discernment regarding God's plans for David. But she also knew that he was on the verge of making a critical error in judgment by taking his own revenge rather than leaving it up to God. Abigail, a master of tact and timing, chose carefully how she would broach sensitive subjects and when she should act on her own initiative. And she chose to stay committed to Nabal rather than run from her problems.

Rather than seeing a woman who loves too much, I see a woman with limited options who exercised the few she had quite effectively. In those days, a woman without a husband had no options. She couldn't obtain a restraining order, find a shelter for battered women, get a job and start a new life. Back then, a wife belonged to her husband in the same way that he "owned" his slaves and his cattle, and he was free to do with her as he wished. Had Abigail left Nabal, she would have been totally without support and protection, and Nabal could have killed or severely punished her if he caught up with her. The option of leaving was not available to her.

However, Abigail still had the option of choosing how she would respond to her circumstances. She never used her husband's boorish behavior as an excuse to act the same way. Rather, she kept growing in a positive direction, so that when the moment of crisis came, she was ready with the skills and spiritual maturity to handle it. Because she had been exercising her inner options, the moment of crisis also became a moment of opportunity—an opportunity to save her family and to be an influence for good in the life of a great man of God.

It's not only difficult marriages that cause the backdrop of some people's lives to be so black. For others it is chronic pain, depression or a physical disability. For some it's a painful childhood memory or a past mistake. It could be a child, a spouse or an in-law who is a constant source of emotional pain. Maybe there is something in life that hurts so badly they've begged the Lord to take it away, but it's still there.

At some point all of us face difficulties that cause deep pain and seem unfixable. Sometimes we wonder if we're going to make it through or if we're going to fly to pieces. In the midst of the unfixables of life, we ask, "How can I be with God in the midst of this? Where is God and does he even care about what I am going through? How can I allow the beauty of the Christ-life to emerge against the backdrop of this difficulty—rather than allowing it to become a black hole that just sucks me into the darkness? How can I experience the freedom Christ offers me when I feel so overwhelmed and trapped in my pain?"

We may not have answers to every dark situation we're in, but we can find ways to open ourselves to God's activity in the midst of our struggle.

Allow yourself to be honest with God. One thing is true: God has the power to change our circumstances. The story of Abigail tells us that. And it is perfectly acceptable for us to ask him to do just that. Paul asked the Lord three times to take away his "thorn in the flesh" (see 2 Corinthians 12:7). Christ prayed the night before he was crucified, "My Father, if it is possible, let this cup pass from me; yet not what I want but what you want" (Matthew 26:39). Even in their willingness to do God's will, they expressed their desire for God to take the hard thing away. This kind of desire is not condemned or forbidden by God.

In the case of both Paul and Christ, God chose not to grant their requests. But that did not lessen the importance of expressing it to him. They still needed to be in communication, to open up their truest questions, and to experience God's presence with them in the midst of their pain and grief and frustration. To understand the importance of this dynamic in our relationship with God, we might think of our relationship with our children. Even when we have to say no to a request, we're not upset that they asked. We still want to talk and to tell them that we care and that they are not alone. Sometimes we are able to offer another perspective or a ray of hope, and sometimes we aren't. But knowing that we're in it together becomes a comfort and a bond. So it is with God. We talk to him first of all because he is our most intimate friend and we want to share all things with him. And that is how relationships develop.

We also talk to him because he has the power to take our pain away; we express our faith and trust in his goodness when we make our requests known to him. Even when he doesn't respond exactly as we would like, we might find that turning to God in the midst of difficulty has a way of kick-starting our relationship with him into a new gear. Remembering the worst storms of her difficult marriage, one woman recalls, "I had a choice between talking to myself or talking to God, so I chose to talk to God. He became like my husband in a way, and as I look back on those times, my relationship with God seemed so much closer than it does now that I'm through the storm."

A difficult marriage or any other kind of hardship gives us the opportunity to learn to trust God and love him despite the circumstances of life. In so doing, we move beyond the honeymoon stage of our faith ("I'll follow God as long as things are going well") to a more mature relationship that transcends hardship and is able to trust even through dark times.

SHE [ABIGAIL] DID NOT ALLOW THE CIRCUMSTANCES OF HER LIFE TO DETERMINE WHAT SHE WOULD BECOME. RATHER THAN BECOMING HARD, BITTER, CYNICAL OR STAGNANT, SHE ALLOWED GOD TO CHISEL AWAY AT HER CHARACTER, MAKING HER BRILLIANTLY BEAUTIFUL AGAINST THE DARK BACKGROUND OF A DIFFICULT LIFE.

Allow difficulties to produce character. It would be easy for us to let the fact that God delivered Abigail from her difficult marriage take our focus off other important facets of this story. For me, the main point is not that she was delivered but that she did not allow the circumstances of her life to determine what she would become. Rather than becoming hard, bitter, cynical or stagnant, she allowed God to chisel away at her character, making her brilliantly beautiful against the dark background of a difficult life.

Interestingly enough, the character qualities that Abigail's circumstances produced in her life were precisely the ones she needed in order to deal with her crisis. These qualities were so much a part of who she was that she didn't even need to stop and think. Undoubtedly, years of living with a difficult man had given her plenty of opportunity to develop the wisdom, tact and courage it took to approach

David effectively. And years of talking with God kept her so in tune with what he was doing in her world that she could offer a spiritual perspective when it was needed. She had not allowed the negative forces in her life to shape her, but rather she allowed them to produce godly character.

Just as physical muscles are developed in the hard work of pulling or pushing against weight or gravity, so our spiritual muscles are developed in the hard work of living in less-than-perfect circumstances. Some character traits can be developed no other way. Romans 5:3-4 says, "We also exult in our tribulations, knowing that tribulation brings about perseverance; and perseverance, proven character; and proven character, hope" (NASB).

Allow difficulties to bond you with others. One of the most profound experiences of my life was accompanying a friend into the delivery room where she gave birth to a baby girl who was too young to survive outside the womb. It was an intense human drama: what is usually a life-giving process produced death. For a few suspended moments we gazed unabashedly into each other's souls, bound together by vulnerability and shared pain. Life and death were there, so closely intertwined. And the tears were there as, together, we grieved the loss of this baby who was already greatly loved. But there was also trust and hope in the Lord that was deeper than words. And even in her pain, I saw beauty and strength in my friend that were different from any physical attribute I had ever seen. Her choice to allow me to be with her in that moment was one of the most valuable gifts I have ever been given.

Everyone has pain and difficulty, but usually we try to keep it hidden for as long as possible. What a loss that is to all of us, because opening up our pain to others can level the ground between us as human beings and allow us to see each other more clearly. Tim Hansel discovered this through the ongoing physical pain he experiences as the result of a climbing accident: "Pain, if allowed, produces an identification with the sufferings of others, and even the sufferings of Christ, that we could not experience any other way. One is allowed to see dignity in the midst of human struggle and see beyond the false barriers that are oftentimes imposed between human beings."

When we experience pain—whether it is the pain of a difficult marriage or any number of other hardships—we have a choice about whether to experience it in isolation or to open it up and find the bond it can create with others. If we are struggling in some area of our life, we can be sure that others are as well. Although often our first response is to offer advice, advice isn't always the best form of support. Usually what a sufferer needs most is the strength and courage that come from knowing we're not alone and that others have their struggles as well. When we make the choice to share our pain, the beauty and strength we see in each other are nothing less than inspiring!

Allow God to be strong through your weakness. One thing I have learned along the way in my life as a writer and spiritual companion is that people don't really want to hear about all the things I've got nailed down and no longer struggle with in life. A life that looks like it's all put together may be motivating to some, but to normal folks it just seems overwhelming and unattainable. As a wise leader wrote, "It's easier to take up a cause led by a fellow human being than to follow someone who covers all signs of weakness." It's not easy to let others see our difficulties and the areas where we are not strong. It seems more natural to hide those things than to risk misunderstanding, embarrassment or disrespect from those who don't know how to respond to human limitations—theirs and ours!

I've come to accept and expect that God will often use areas of weakness and vulnerability in my life—even the areas I'm ashamed of!—for his purposes. Of course I would like to put only my strengths out there for everyone to see. Wouldn't we all? But God has a different plan. Again we can learn from the apostle Paul and his own thorn in the flesh. He says that God wants us to "boast" about our weaknesses, in other words, put them right out there in plain view so that God's power can come shining through.

Even when God does say, "No, I'm not going to take the pain away for reasons that only I know right now," as we talk with him about it, he gives us the opportunity to take a step back and look at the larger picture. Sometimes he even allows us to understand his reasons. Although we can never completely understand the mind of God on these matters, we do know some things.

First of all, we know that pain and weakness keep us in touch with our vulnerability and in touch with our need for God and others. As Paul learned through his thorn in the flesh, pride lurks in dark corners of our hearts. Often the greater the work that God is doing in and through our life, the more susceptible to pride we are. Paul realized this: "To keep me from exalting myself, there was given me a thorn in the flesh, a messenger of Satan to torment me—to keep me from exalting myself" (2 Corinthians 12:7 NASB). Another truth Paul realized was that his thorn in the flesh would keep him available as a means by which God could show his power. One pastor put it this way: "When we are truly in touch with our ordinariness, we become vulnerable, and [this very weakness] becomes a black velvet background against which the stunning diamond of the power of God is seen pouring through our lives."

WHEN THE GOING GETS *TOO* TOUGH

As inspiring as Abigail's story is, it is important for us to realize that there is a difference between "good hard" and "destructive hard." God calls us to remain in the midst of some difficulties—difficulties that transform us over time in ways that are beyond imagining. One friend, who lost her eighteen-year-old daughter in a car accident, held me in a tight hug several weeks after her loss and whispered in my ear, "I am not the same!" Her voice had a sense of awe and gratitude, a "given-overness" to God. Rather than going the way of soul-numbing bitterness, she was allowing God to do his transforming work in her through this terribly hard thing.

Another kind of "hard" needs to be acknowledged here, the kind of difficulty that is dark and evil and begins to tear at the very fabric of our soul. Violence and abuse of any kind—particularly domestic violence—are the "destructive hard" that we have the right to war against and flee from for our own good and for the good of those around us.

Domestic violence is the greatest single cause of injury to American women—more than auto accidents, rape, and mugging combined. These facts have led some to conclude that home is the most dangerous place a woman can be. With this in mind, I want to clarify that *in no way do I wish my comments in this chapter to be construed as encouragement for any woman to stay in an abusive relationship.*

Spousal abuse is a sin before God and a crime punishable by law. It is, without exception, intolerable. No woman should be encouraged to think that domestic violence is normal or what she deserves. The idea that if a woman would behave differently she could placate the violent man in her life is a trap. In actuality, violence is "a specific choice made by the abusive husband. If frustrating situations offered only one option, abusers would be equally violent on the job, driving in traffic or interacting with friends; but it is simply not true. The majority of abusers direct their violence specifically and purposefully toward their wives." In many cases, the more compliant and submissive a woman becomes, the more violent her husband gets. And once a pattern of violence has been established, it will continue until there is some sort of crisis (such as the wife leaving, an intervention, or an arrest).

It would be comforting to think that in Christian marriages these problems do not exist, but this simply is not the case. Phyllis Alsdurf prepared an article for *FamilyLife Today* on wife abuse in Christian homes and was stunned at the magnitude of the problem: "Wives told of being struck in the face, kicked, bruised, dragged across the floor by their hair, and even bitten. And by whom? Ordained ministers, Christian businessmen, some well-known evangelical leaders— all men who lived a lie and perpetuated abuse that was an abomination to God."

The response to her article convinced Phyllis and her husband, James (a clinical and forensic psychologist), that this problem was more common among Christians than they had ever realized. It prompted them to spend eight years researching and writing the book *Battered into Submission,* in which they document the problem of wife abuse among Christians and trace some of its major roots to faulty theology taught in many fundamentalist homes and churches. They observe that "the distribution of power can be badly skewed in the Christian home. Fortified by preaching that accepts all sort of cultural assumptions about what 'headship' means, abusers often use Scripture as ammunition for their misuse of power."

One battered wife explained how her husband's (and her own!) theology contributed to the abuse she had suffered:

> After marriage, my husband treated me as a nonperson with no value other than through him. He cited Scripture passages in

support of his treatment of me. Any time I objected to his behavior or to his decisions, he told me that I was to submit to
him just as totally as if he were Jesus Christ. He firmly believed
that if I were obedient and submissive, God himself would take
care of me. Therefore he was free to behave as irresponsibly as
he liked without fear of hurting me or our child. He felt God
wouldn't allow us to be hurt unless it was God's will.

My husband took no responsibility for his actions at all. I
spent many hours in prayer and fasting, seeking to drive out
every vestige of sin from my life. I believed that when I finally
learned what God was trying to teach me, my husband would
respond with love. But the more I submitted to him, the more
arrogantly he displayed his flagrant abusive behavior. I sought
counsel from pastors and friends. Many didn't believe me. It's
not hard to understand why. How could such an upstanding
member of the church and community be capable of such a
miscarriage of God's justice? . . . Those who did believe me offered no solace; only sympathy and empty platitudes. They affirmed my submissive reaction to my husband's abusive
tyranny. No one at any time went to talk to my husband about
his behavior in loving correction. I was always left empty-
handed to return to my own personal hell.

It is easy to see how the sin of wife abuse can go unchecked in circles where wives are taught to submit blindly to husbands, where divorce is preached against without any consideration given to circumstances, and where dominance by the husband is seen as his divine
right and responsibility. In fact, such teachings provide good cover
for abuse under the guise of bringing one's wife "into subjection."
Thus the batterer does not consider his actions abusive; he is simply

fulfilling his God-given responsibilities.

Wife abuse is a symptom of deeper problems in the marriage—low self-esteem, poor problem-solving and conflict-resolution skills, not knowing how to cope with intense emotion, patterns of violence learned in childhood, and so on. However, "it is too dangerous to discuss the problems of marriage until everyone is safe. Any problems with conflict resolution or communication cannot be realistically discussed while the husband is blatantly abusing power. Trust and confidence cannot be developed unless safety is achieved first."

A battered woman's first step, then, is to gain safety for herself and for her children. She can do this through calling a local domestic violence hotline or a women's shelter. If a hotline does not exist, calling 911 and asking for the number of a local domestic violence agency can also be effective. A woman must believe that she and her children are worth a better life (no small feat for a woman whose husband has been demeaning her for years) and be willing to do any or all of the following to get it: call the police, press assault charges, leave and refuse to consider returning until the abuser has completed a counseling program for offenders, or go public with the abuse to employers, relatives and the church community. This is the means by which "a woman offers her husband yet another opportunity to acknowledge the illegality and immorality of what he has done. These are acts of both self-preservation and love for her husband. Since he is participating in evil, forcing him to deal with it and not submitting to it is an act of love."

The Alsdurfs are quick to point out, however, that once a victim has taken the first step, she holds virtually no power over whether the batterer will choose the path of true reconciliation. While expressing confidence in the power of God's love to redeem relationships characterized by abuse, they acknowledge that most often reconciliation does not occur. When it does, it is not an event but a painful and slow process that involves more than willpower. For the abuser, it involves facing the horror of his sin, confessing it (both privately and publicly), expressing his intent to change, and committing himself to the process of learning new patterns for loving and relating to his family. This is accomplished through professional therapy, support groups and strong accountability within a community of Christians. For the abused, it involves forgiving, not primarily for his sake but for her own. There is no easy way back, but there is a way. But it will never happen unless someone has the courage to say, "Enough."

A Fork in the Road

"Life is difficult," says M. Scott Peck in the opening line of *The Road Less Traveled*. He goes on to say that this is a great truth because "once we accept this truth, we transcend it. . . . Because once it is accepted, the fact that life is difficult no longer matters." What does matter is what we do with it.

The difficulties and pains of our lives bring us to a fork in the road, a place where we must choose. And it's impossible to stay neutral. To allow our pain and difficulty to corrode our spirit, to make us hard and bitter, is to have chosen. To keep living for some future escape is to refuse the present. To allow God to transform us in the situation as we are honest with him, as we invite his perspective, as we deal forthrightly with our difficulties, and as we open our lives to others in strength and vulnerability—this is the road less traveled. And choosing that road will make all the difference.

Spiritual Exercises

Alone with God

Silence. As you come to the end of this chapter, take a few moments to sit with God in the silence of your heart and allow yourself to become aware of the area in your life that seems like it is unfixable. Allow the full gravity of your situation and all the emotions that you feel to come to the surface of your heart and mind. Don't try to fix anything or figure anything out. Just be with God right where you are; rest in him and allow him to comfort you as a parent would comfort a child.

Prayer and journaling. Review what you have just read in this chapter, noticing the places of resonance and resistance that you have highlighted. Allow yourself the time to reflect on and journal about your experiences and longings. Tell God what's true about you right now and what you long for. Then listen for his response.

- How did you feel as you read about Abigail?
- How is your situation the same or different?
- Who is God for you in the midst of this difficulty?
- What questions would you like to ask him?
- How is God using your difficulty to shape you and bless others?
- How do you feel when you think about putting your areas of weakness out front for others to see?
- Is your difficulty in the "good hard" category or is it in the "destructive hard" category?

Invitations. God, are you inviting me to do anything in response to this chapter? How are you calling me to respond?

CHAPTER TEN

Reaching Across Generations

If the truth be told, we today are who we are—if we are anybody—
because some woman, somewhere, stooped down long enough that we might
climb on her back and ride piggyback into the future.

RENITA WEEMS, *JUST A SISTER AWAY*

Perhaps you are familiar with the term *doublespeak*. Doublespeak is the practice of obscuring the unpleasantness of a subject by couching it in euphemistic terms. My personal favorite is the travel newsletter that refers to the over-sixty crowd not as senior citizens but as the "chronologically gifted." The reason I like this one is that, rather than obscuring the truth, this phrase actually clarifies a truth that would otherwise be lost: older people *are* "chronologically gifted" with wisdom they have gained from weathering the seasons of life.

I have had the privilege of being in several life-changing relationships with women who are "chronologically gifted." In fact, as I look back over my spiritual development and try to pinpoint the factors that have influenced me the most, I seldom think of a particular Bible study or sermon. Instead I often think of older women who have

spent time sharing their lives with me that have had the most significant role in my spiritual transformation.

Ruth Anne had been a close friend of our family for years. Realizing that even the best training at home needs to be supplemented by
the input of other gifted Christians, my parents arranged for me to
spend one of my college summers with Ruth Anne and her husband.
Though I spent most of that summer working in a fast-food restaurant, it was one of the richest times of my life spiritually. Ruth Anne
memorized Scripture a book at a time, so I memorized too. She gave
me a copy of A. W. Tozer's *Knowledge of the Holy,* which helped deepen
my relationship with God. Every evening we went for a three-mile

> AS I LOOK BACK OVER MY SPIRITUAL DEVELOPMENT
> AND TRY TO PINPOINT THE FACTORS THAT HAVE
> INFLUENCED ME THE MOST, I SELDOM THINK OF A
> PARTICULAR BIBLE STUDY OR SERMON. INSTEAD IT IS
> OLDER WOMEN WHO HAVE SPENT TIME SHARING THEIR
> LIVES WITH ME THAT HAVE HAD THE MOST SIGNIFI-
> CANT ROLE IN MY SPIRITUAL TRANSFORMATION.

walk in the Virginia hills surrounding their home and talked about
everything from boyfriends to church government to the problem
passages in Hebrews. She allowed me just to live and learn with her,
and that summer was life changing. Later, I returned to her home for
a week-long visit with my husband and three children. During that
visit much of our conversation revolved around childrearing. I articulated some of my fears and uncertainties; she made some observa-
tions and offered me encouragement, instruction and resources. It
was just the kind of challenge I needed!

Darlene shared her life with me in a different way. While I was in college, far from my own family, she took an interest in me and invited me to her home quite often. Our relationship was characterized by commitment, open sharing and prayer. I saved all my deep and not-so-deep questions for our get-togethers. Her perspective was a treasured source of help and encouragement. As an older woman, she was able to teach me so much through the friendship she allowed to develop between us.

SHARING TRUTH

Of course, the idea of older women helping younger women is not a new one. It is a biblical principle that often gets lost in the shuffle from this meeting to that Bible study. Titus 2:3-5 instructs older women to be reverent in their behavior "so that they may encourage the young women to love their husbands, to love their children, to be self-controlled, chaste, good managers of the household, kind, being submissive to their husbands, so that the word of God may not be discredited." A few key point stand out to me in this passage.

Life experience rather than age. Paul does not define the age groups to which he is referring when he uses the words *older* and *younger.* He doesn't say, "Older women are those who have reached some magical age when they are suddenly deemed mature." This lack of definition indicates that all of us can be teaching and learning from each other back and forth on a continuum, rather than seeing ourselves in rigid age categories. What qualifies us to teach others is maturity and life experience rather than chronological age.

Showing first rather than telling. The apostle is speaking here of a type of ministry in which you show it with your life before you tell it with your mouth. Paul's use of the word *encourage,* which can be translated "teach what is good," indicates teaching by example as well as verbal instruction. Paul's own life and writings illustrate how he helped younger Christians to maturity through relationships characterized by affection, tender care and fatherly encouragement (1 Thessalonians 2:7-11). He opened up his very life so that others could learn from his example. And when it was necessary, he expressed his love through confrontation with tears (2 Corinthians 2:4). He knew that we do not necessarily need more Bible studies or preaching services; we need relationships that provide examples to follow.

MOST YOUNG WOMEN DO NOT NEED ANOTHER MOTHER, THEY JUST NEED AN OLDER FRIEND.

Encouragement rather than mothering. Most young women do not need another mother, they just need an older friend. Win Couchman gives an effective image of the role of the older woman with the image of one car following another in a deep fog. The tail lights ahead helped her increase her speed from 15 to 25 miles per hour. The two cars had no official relationship—the followers didn't ask to get in the other car or be hooked up with a tow rope. They were just following along behind someone who was a little farther along and who could light the way. In fact, the driver of the car in front probably didn't even realize anyone was following! But unknowingly, she or he was providing just the amount of light that was needed.

BUT CAN IT WORK TODAY?

This idea sounds so logical, so right, so comfortable. It conjures up images of a world where women share their experiences as they sit quilting or baking bread together—a world that, for most of us, is long gone.

Our world, by contrast, is transient, fast paced and filled with new challenges for women. Young women today tend to move across country instead of across town and find themselves cut off from their mothers and other women whom they have known and learned from all their lives. And the older women find themselves with very empty nests indeed. In addition, the number of working women has increased so dramatically that the networking that used to occur quite naturally no longer takes place. The woman who chooses to stay at home full time may find herself the only one home in her neighborhood during the day. In the meantime, working women find that they are barely holding themselves and their family together, without much energy or time for mutually beneficial relationships. Ironically, these very differences cause us to need such helping relationships now more than ever.

Incorporating this timeless principle of intergenerational friendships into contemporary life is possible if we are willing to be flexible and customize. There is no precise formula for helping relationships to grow, because friendships are as diverse as personalities themselves. Some women get together to study the Bible and pray, while others meet more spontaneously as situations arise. Sometimes a young woman may ask an older woman to share an area of expertise: some aspect of childrearing, entertaining, interior decorating or professional advice. When a young woman is struggling with something specific, such as job stress, communication in marriage, sexual purity, materialism or jealousy, she might approach an older woman to help her in that area. Some women begin with a time limit in mind; others continue indefinitely with periods of varying intensity. No matter what your stage in life, these relationships can be customized to meet the needs and lifestyles of those involved.

SETTING THE TONE FOR CROSS-GENERATIONAL RELATIONSHIPS

One of the most important things we can do to facilitate cross-generational relationships is to give some attention to our mindset. Certain pervasive social attitudes make it very difficult for women to encourage and learn from each other. Sometimes these attitudes exist and are conveyed to others unbeknownst to us, but their presence can greatly hinder mutually beneficial relationships.

One of the biggest barriers to relationships between women today is younger women's attitude of self-sufficiency. While it is good for women to have a sense of their personal accountability before God so as not to be overly swayed by the opinions of others, there is a kind of independence that can be counterproductive. This independence is rooted in pride, and it results in a disregard for the counsel of others who are older and wiser.

It isn't always easy for today's younger woman to learn from someone else—we're a pretty independent group! Never before have women been able to enjoy such success in careers and other achievements, and it is exhilarating. But a growing self-confidence can easily translate into a false sense of control over one's life in which there is no need for anyone's help. We have allowed images of the professional woman who is out there "putting her best foot forward" to become our model for success.

These attitudes can carry over into our spiritual life, and we can find ourselves maintaining the impression that we are attractive, poised, gifted and spiritually mature. We maintain this image even during times of great difficulty, so that it becomes almost impossible for us to accept help, encouragement or training from older women. Of course, older women sense these attitudes and feel that we do not want or need their help. Then when times of need do cause us to be more open, the older women are nowhere to be found.

I was at such a juncture after the birth of my second child. My husband and I had withdrawn from a lot of our activities because of increased family responsibilities. I was not recovering very quickly and was feeling lonely and overwhelmed; my self-sufficiency gave way to frightening feelings of isolation. I was desperate for friendship, encouragement and practical help from older women, but none was forthcoming. At first I was angry. I assumed that these women were neglecting their responsibilities. But as I began to probe for reasons, I was told that people thought I had it all together and didn't need their help. Ironically enough, that is what I had wanted them to think. But now my carefully tended image of a confident, poised, self-sufficient young woman had backfired! It had made me unapproachable and beyond the reach of those who would have liked to offer encouragement.

Through this experience I discovered a dichotomy within myself. A part of me recognized my need for support and encouragement, but another part of me wanted to continue appearing totally competent and self-assured. I believe other young women experience the same inner struggle, and it is important for us to deal with the pride that can become a barrier between us and the older women whose encouragement we need.

If we want relationships with older women to flourish, we need to guard against being wise in our own eyes (Proverbs 3:7)—so wise that we disregard the wisdom of others. We need to communicate to more mature women that they have a lot to offer and that we would greatly benefit from time spent with them. We must learn to listen and be open to what they are saying even when it hurts—when our first reaction is to get defensive and back away. Developing a teachable attitude and accepting older women as role models may require a change for some of us. However, women who are humble and teachable are the ones who are growing and learning.

Older women can also be responsible for attitudes that are hidden enemies of fruitful relationships. When they allow themselves to pass judgment on younger women—even if that judgment is unspoken—the perceptive woman will sense this and not risk opening up. Marsha has genuine love and concern for younger women, demonstrated by her willingness to invest time and energy in relationships with them. However, she has a low tolerance for new ideas and has difficulty understanding women whose struggles are different from her own. Consequently, when she reaches a point of disagreement with a younger woman, she withdraws her friendship and moves on to someone else who sees things more her way. She has had a string of friendships that follow this pattern, and several women have been deeply hurt. The following guidelines can help prevent this unhealthy kind of relationship.

Keep the goal in relationships clearly in mind. Those of us who are considered to be more experienced are responsible to encourage others by our example and verbal instruction. We are not to make others into carbon copies of ourselves or force them to make the same choices we have made in order to win our approval. It is good to remember that they are not accountable to us but to God. As Romans 14:4 says, "Who are you to pass judgment on servants of another? It is before their own lord that they stand or fall. And they will be upheld, for the Lord is able to make them stand." It is our responsibility to offer ourselves in relationships; it is God's responsibility to bring about growth and change.

Don't give too much advice too soon. Too often we offer advice before giving younger women the chance to express themselves fully. This is unfortunate, because the very process of expressing feelings and talking through one's problems can be therapeutic. Learning to ask thoughtful questions will take us a long way in understanding what the other person is experiencing: "How does that make you feel? What is it that you really want? How do you think that decision will affect those closest to you? Has God brought any Scripture to mind regarding this decision?" Often a woman can find her own answers if she is given time to verbalize her concerns and brainstorm a little. Also, if we do not take the time to listen first, we run the risk of giving answers that are simplistic or irrelevant. It is no wonder the Bible says, "If one gives answer before hearing, it is folly and shame" (Proverbs 18:13).

MUTUAL TRANSFORMATION

In my experience, the best cross-generational relationships are those in which both the younger woman and the older woman are contributing to each other. No relationship is as healthy as it could be if it indefinitely remains all taking and no giving. Relationships characterized by an awareness that each has something to give and something to gain are invigorating rather than draining. They tend to last long after any formal arrangements for the relationship have fallen away. The age difference is not disregarded or forgotten, but both women come to understand that chronological age does not define what we have to offer one another.

My friendship with another Ruth has been marked by this kind of mutuality. Our relationship began somewhat typically—she was an elder's wife at the church we attended. Many young women were drawn to her because of her honesty, compassion and obvious spiritual depth. When I accepted the responsibility of directing the women's ministry, I asked Ruth if she would be willing to be a part of the women's ministry leadership team because I knew her teaching and pastoral gifts would be a real asset. I asked her if she would meet with me regularly to pray, to offer her input and perspective and to be supportive on a very personal level. I was delighted when she agreed, and thus began a friendship that has endured through challenges that neither one of us could have imagined at the outset.

Some of those challenges were related to the fact that she was an elder's wife in the church where I became a staff member. When staff and elders came down on different sides of an issue, it was awkward and stressful. Other challenges had to do with personality and generational differences. I was very direct in my communication and ready to plow ahead on issues that she needed to take more slowly. We both suffered because of gender inequities in the church, but she expressed her suffering through tears and sadness (which is generally more acceptable for women), and I expressed mine through anger, which was hard for her to deal with at times. We were at different stages in our lives, so she could not take some of the risks I was free to take. This was disappointing, but we loved and respected each other enough to accept that God was leading us down our individual paths.

It took us awhile to learn that we were different—but one was not better than the other. We went through some painful transitions in our life together at church—disagreeing vehemently at times—but we learned to negotiate those rough spots with honesty, mutual respect, commitment to the relationship that transcended issues, and giving each other space when we needed it. Our relationship became so valuable to both of us that we found ourselves determined not to let anything destroy it. Now that Ruth has moved away and some of the outside pressures on our relationship have been removed, I marvel at what we made it through.

What did we offer one another that was worth such an investment of time and emotional energy? For me, this relationship was honest on deeper levels than any relationship I had ever had with an older woman (other than my own mother). Ruth went through some very deep waters during the time we were meeting on a regular basis, and she was remarkably vulnerable in opening them up for me. She made no attempt to conceal her struggles or make them seem easier than they were. She had no simplistic solutions. The lessons I learned from seeing the unvarnished version of her experiences, from weeping with her and praying for her, will be with me for the rest of my life. She led by example, freeing me to share some of my most personal struggles as well. This vulnerability—which manifested itself in her friendships, her leadership style and her teaching—had a significant impact on my own friendships and ministry style.

In addition, her graciousness in accepting and following the leadership of this young whippersnapper (which is what I was) gave me tremendous confidence. Knowing that she believed in me helped me believe in myself. I was amazed at her willingness to learn from me even though I was her junior by about fifteen years. We shared information, and both of us were open to being stretched by the new ideas and ways of looking at the world that we were picking up in our study and other relationships. We were also able to be open about what was going on in the relationship: feelings of competitiveness, disappointment, anger, intimidation, being misunderstood. Our honesty was painful at times, but because our love and commitment were never in question, we were able to use these experiences to gain a deeper understanding of ourselves as well as each other.

It has always been obvious what I, the younger woman, gained in this friendship. But Ruth listed in a letter some things I had given her as well:

- A cross-generational relationship, which I so much need [in order] to understand myself, my daughters, the world, God.

- A desire for honest assessment of life and its foundational principles.

- An open delving into a very difficult area of life . . . revealing your hurts, listening to and absorbing mine.

- Opposite perspective or a "different" (not wrong) way of viewing a predicament.

- Patience in accepting me and trying to understand my limits of conscience and actions due to prior commitments.

- Vulnerability and truth-telling.

- Steadfastness to continue the relationship when we hit hard and tall barriers in the church setting and, at times, found ourselves almost on opposite sides, staring through at each other.

- The largeness of spirit to admit defeat and at other times to say, "I'm sorry. Forgive me."

- The example of preparing clearly [to take a stand] and then opening your mouth to verbalize it. This has given me more courage.

- The joy of having another woman beside me committed to the Scriptures.

- Much hope that honest relationships can be built as you have not let me go, nor have I let you go . . . because we have weathered each other's "hard" counsel at times, asked forgiveness, explained ourselves, tried to understand each other, recognized that we are different but are both needed in the kingdom, and that we need each other.

This was not a perfect relationship. It didn't happen at the perfect time, the perfect place, in the perfect way or with two perfect people. It was not without its mistakes. But it happened with commitment, honesty and mutuality—some of the best stuff we as women have to give each other. Together we learned that women who uphold each other become more powerful.

GETTING STARTED

All of us have opportunities to know someone younger than ourselves who could benefit from time spent with us and someone older than ourselves from whom we could learn. As we begin to realize our responsibility to those younger than ourselves, we can ask God to show us someone in whom we can invest our time. A relatively young woman can keep her eyes open for a high school or college girl who seems open to her input. Meet somewhere for a Coke. Or if your schedule is crowded, invite her to go along with you while you shop or take your kids to the park. All of us can be sensitive to "divine appointments" and use situations in which we are thrown together with younger women (such as nursery duty, committee work, or traveling to a conference or retreat) as opportunities to take a special interest in them.

As younger women, we can take the initiative to identify women we respect and actively pursue friendships with them. We can let the relationships unfold naturally or ask them to consider meeting with us on a regular basis. Taking the attitude of a learner will make it easier for older women to share their lives with us. Realizing that we each have something to offer in relationships, regardless of our age and stage, will encourage us to search out and cultivate friendships that are mutually fulfilling.

I've heard it said, "If you can't be a good example, then you'll just have to be a terrible warning." That's a frightening prospect! God's idea is for older women to be good examples of how he transforms everyday life—how he helps us build up our family by loving our husband and children properly, how he helps us develop strong character, make right personal choices and avoid the pitfalls that are so abundant these days. It's the real stuff of life that can't be learned in a classroom but is best learned by watching someone else. Even in our transient, fast-paced society, he wants us to be always reaching ahead to learn from those who are farther along in their journey and reaching back to those who are coming along behind. With God's help, we can become the encouraging, nonjudgmental, teachable women who can make it happen.

SPIRITUAL EXERCISES

Alone with God

Silence. As you come to the end of this chapter, take a few moments to sit with God in the silence of your heart. Who has reached across the generations to provide guidance for your journey into spiritual transformation? Allow yourself to experience gratitude for the gift that this woman has been to you.

Prayer and journaling. Review what you have just read in this chapter, noticing the places of resonance and resistance that you have highlighted. Tell God what's true about you right now and what you long for. Then listen for his response.

- What are your hopes, dreams or longings for the kind of relationship described in this chapter?

- Do you have any previous experiences that cause you to doubt the possibilities or to be open to the possibilities?

- Is God speaking to you about any attitude that might need to shift in order for you to engage in this kind of relationship?

Invitations. God, are you inviting me to respond in some way to what I have read today?

CHAPTER ELEVEN

Being Christ in the World

Sooner or later, if we follow Christ we have to risk everything in order
to gain everything. We have to gamble on the invisible and risk all that we
see and taste and feel. But we know the risk is worth it, because there is
nothing more insecure than this transient world.

THOMAS MERTON, *THOUGHTS IN SOLITUDE*

These are exciting and challenging days for women, days full of choice and opportunity. Controversies continue over the roles of women and men in marriage, ministry and the marketplace, and the issues that have been raised will not go away. Their complexity demands that we continue in the spiritual practices and relationships that open us to true wisdom and discernment. The disciplines of solitude and silence, Scripture reflection, prayer and spiritual friendship will help us hear and respond to the One True Voice in the midst of conflicting voices and expectations. Even as we move beyond the limits that others impose on us and seek to nurture a world in which the strengths of women can fully emerge, that Voice reminds us that our deepest calling is to allow the transformations of the Christ-life to unfold uniquely in us.

It is here that we part company with the feminist for whom the fight for fairness and equality has become an end in itself. It is here that our lives might become an uncomfortable challenge to women for whom personal comfort, keeping the peace or maintaining the status quo have become the highest value. Here we choose not to look to the lives of others as a blueprint for our own but dare to say yes to the risky invitations of God. As Jesus told the apostle Peter when Peter compared himself and his calling to that of the apostle John, "If it is my will that he [John] remain until I come, what is that to you? Follow me!" (John 21:22).

As we respond to Christ's invitation to follow him, we learn from his example, letting ourselves be transformed by the truth and the freedom he lived.

CHRIST GAVE HIMSELF FREELY TO THE WILL OF GOD

Actually Christ was in a situation similar to that which women often face: for the most part, he was not recognized for who he was or what he had to offer. Yet the main purpose of his life was not to prove who he was or to glorify himself. He knew who he was in relation to God and humankind. He knew that he was here to do God's will in God's timing and that at the proper time his full identity and purpose would be revealed. In the meantime, he moved through life with single-mindedness unaffected by the opinion or persuasion of others.

Early in his ministry, when Satan, the disciples and even his family members tried to convince him to reveal his identity and set up his kingdom, Jesus refused to be pushed. His answer was always some variation on the statement he made to his brothers when they encouraged him to show himself to the world at one of the Jewish festivals: "Go to the festival yourselves. I am not going to this festival, for my time has not yet fully come" (John 7:8).

When Peter first heard about Jesus' impending death and pro-
tested the necessity of it—"God forbid it, Lord! This must never happen to you!"—Jesus refused to be sidetracked from the main purpose
for which he had come. "Get behind me, Satan! You are a stumbling
block to me; for you are setting your mind not on divine things but
on human things" (Matthew 16:22-23).

When the Pharisees and religious leaders began to persecute him
and try to arrest him, he was undeterred because he knew that ultimately God's will would be accomplished through him, regardless of
human interference. Sometimes he withdrew for a while, but never
for very long. He always came back, faithfully ministering, healing
and speaking the message that people needed to hear.

I am tremendously comforted as well as challenged by this image
of an unflappable Christ walking this earth with an unwavering commitment "to do the will of him who sent me" (John 4:34). He expected that those who didn't understand what he was trying to do
would attempt to stop him—some out of ignorance and some out of
malice. But because he was in such close communion with the Father
and knew he was in the center of his will, peace emanated from him.

GOD DOES NOT WASTE HIS GIFTS OR HIS CALLING. AS
WE ENGAGE IN THE PROCESS OF SPIRITUAL TRANSFOR-
MATION, HE WILL PLACE US WHERE WE CAN BE OF
GREATEST USE TO HIM.

As we observe this in Christ's life, we too can rest in the fact that
people—even those who try to limit the ways in which women serve

God—cannot ultimately prevent God from accomplishing his will in and through our lives. If he has given me spiritual gifts to use in service to others, he will give me opportunities to use them. Too often we look to people to recognize our gifts and give us opportunities to use them, as if they had ultimate control. But God does not waste his gifts or his calling. As we engage in the process of spiritual transformation, he will place us where we can be of greatest use to him.

CHRIST LEARNED OBEDIENCE THROUGH THE THINGS HE SUFFERED

I am reminded of Joseph, whom God caused to find favor in the eyes of key people so that God's purposes could be accomplished—despite jealous brothers who sold him to strangers, false accusations by an immoral woman and the forgetfulness of a cupbearer. The vision God gave Joseph while he was still a young boy, the lessons he learned while he was second-in-command at Potiphar's house, the breaking he experienced during time in jail and his meteoric rise to the top of Egyptian government were all part of God's plan for him that could not be thwarted. Later in his life he was able to say, without bitterness, to the brothers who had been so cruel, "Even though you intended to do harm to me, God intended it for good, in order to preserve a numerous people" (Genesis 50:20). Like Joseph, we can look past people and situations that seem limiting and see an all-powerful God.

Scripture makes the surprising statement in Hebrews 5:8-9 that Christ "learned obedience through what he suffered; and having been made perfect, he became the source of eternal salvation for all who obey him." To me this statement about the reality and the purpose of Christ's suffering is one of the most amazing and freeing truths about him found in Scripture. It is amazing because it is hard to comprehend why Jesus needed to learn if he was already perfect. At the same time, it is very freeing because it helps me realize that to learn or to have need of learning is nothing to be ashamed of.

This insight into Christ's life became a particular comfort and instruction to me some years ago. I wanted badly to serve on a committee that I cared very much about, and I felt I had the qualifications to make a positive contribution. I expressed my desire to the chairman of the committee but was never invited. I was sure this was because I was a woman and that it was yet another instance where "women had to do twice as well as men to be thought half as good." That may have been partially true, but it wasn't all.

When I got up the nerve to ask the chairman about it, he pointed to weaknesses in my character that he felt would render me ineffective on that committee. These were hard words to hear. But as much as I wanted to run away from his words and categorically deny them, I needed to consider the truth in what he was saying and learn from his feedback. I knew that God wanted me to look past the people in the situation and see him disciplining and training me. The discipline was painful, not pleasant (as it says in Hebrews 12:11), but I needed it.

Our suffering cannot be compared with Christ's—given the intensity of Christ's suffering and the fact that ours is often connected with our character weaknesses—yet it is encouraging to know that we are in very good company as we try to remain open to learning. Hebrews makes it clear that the things Christ learned through his suffering prepared him to be our perfect Savior—One who could understand what it means to suffer in obedience to God. Even though he was fully divine, there were some things he needed to learn through experience. How much more true this will be for us!

If we want to follow God courageously and live lives that are consistent with the way he has gifted and called us, there will always be this kind of learning to be done. We will seldom get it right the first time, and sometimes there may be consequences to suffer for our mistakes. At other times we will be called upon to suffer for doing what is right (as Christ did) and will have the opportunity to identify with Christ in new ways and grow in fellowship with him (Philippians 3:10). We can be encouraged by Christ's example not to become hardened and immovable in our approach to life but rather to relax into the process of growing and learning.

CHRIST WAS FULL OF GRACE AND TRUTH

Nothing got Christ into trouble more regularly than his consistency in speaking the truth. It was usually after some particularly honest moment—such as the times he revealed that he was God in the flesh or exposed the hypocrisy of the Pharisees—that crowds got violent, picked up stones to stone him or tried to arrest him. For those whose hearts were open, however, his penetrating insight was one of the things that convinced them of his authenticity as the Son of God.

Although Christ was consistent in telling the truth, he told it in a variety of ways. He chose a communication style that was appropriate for each situation. With the Samaritan woman, Christ was very gentle and at times subtle in helping her understand the truth about who he was, who she was and what she needed. With people like Nicodemus (the Pharisee who came to see Jesus by night in John 3) and the rich young ruler (Mark 10:17), he was polite but cut right to the heart of the matter. In response to Nicodemus's lack of understanding of the fundamentals of the gospel, he said,

> You're a respected teacher of Israel and you don't know these basics? Listen carefully. I'm speaking sober truth to you. I speak only of what I know by experience; I give witness only to what

I have seen with my own eyes. . . . Yet instead of facing the evidence and accepting it, you procrastinate with questions. If I
tell you things that are plain as the hand before your face and
you don't believe me, what use is there in telling you of things
you can't see, the things of God? (John 3:10-12 *The Message*)

To the rich young ruler, who wanted to know what he had to do
to inherit eternal life, Christ had this to say: "You lack one thing; go,
sell what you own, and give the money to the poor, and you will have
treasure in heaven; then come, follow me" (Mark 10:21). Honest.
Take it or leave it. (This guy left it.)

And then there were the religious leaders, for whom Christ re-
served his strongest brand of truth-telling. It seems that politeness
and subtlety would not be effective with ones who were so hard-
headed:

Woe to you Pharisees! For you tithe mint and rue and herbs of
all kinds [they were legalistic to the point of tithing on every last
spice], and neglect justice and the love of God; it is these you
ought to have practiced, without neglecting the others. Woe to
you Pharisees! For you love to have the seat of honor in the synagogues and to be greeted with respect in the marketplaces.
Woe to you! For you are like unmarked graves, and people walk
over them without realizing it. (Luke 11:42-44)

No wonder the Pharisees and scribes began to be hostile toward him.

At times speaking the truth was not enough; action was needed.
For instance, when opportunists used the spiritual yearnings of poor
people as an occasion to make money in the temple courts, Christ became so indignant and impassioned for justice that he strode through
the temple court, overturning their tables and chasing them out

(Matthew 21:12). At that point the blind and the lame practically came out of the woodwork, as though they had been waiting for someone who had pure motives to come and care for them. And Christ healed them. But where were the spiritual leaders with wisdom and courage enough to stand for what was right?

In an earlier chapter, I discussed the particular struggle that women in our culture have with telling the truth or taking a stand. In light of Christ's example, it would seem hard for us to justify cowering in a corner, avoiding telling the truth, when there is hypocrisy or injustice to be exposed. What would Jesus do? He would tell the truth. He would have several different styles from which to choose, and he would pick the one best suited to the situation. But he would do it. And so will we if we are following in his steps.

CHRIST ALLOWED HIMSELF TO BE MOVED WITH COMPASSION

The English language doesn't have a single word to denote Christ's compassion. In fact, in its biblical usage as it relates to Christ's experience, *to have compassion* is a verb that means "to be moved as to one's inwards, to yearn with compassion, to suffer with another, to be affected similarly."

Compassion was not something Christ *had,* it was a moving within. It caused him to weep, to reach out and touch, to heal, to raise from the dead, to cast out demons, to speak the truth that would set the multitudes and the individual free.

When he saw that the crowds were hungry, he was moved with compassion to mobilize his disciples to feed them (Matthew 15:32). When he saw with spiritual eyes the crowds of people like sheep lost without a shepherd, he spoke from a heart filled with compassion and began to teach them many things. He then called his disciples so they could share in this vision, giving them power, authority and a plan so they too could meet needs (Matthew 9:35—10:42). When the rich young ruler came for instruction on how to receive eternal life, Jesus looked at him, loved him and then told him the hard truth (Mark 10:21). When he saw a widow on the way to bury her only son and envisioned what her life would be without him, he was moved with compassion to raise him from the dead (Luke 7:12-15).

One of the most wrenching accounts of Christ's compassion comes during his triumphal entry into Jerusalem. Finally, people were getting the idea that he was the Messiah, and they began waving palm branches and shouting "Hosanna!" or "Save us, we pray!" But as Jesus approached that beloved city, he saw the tragedy that was in its future. Rather than being caught up in this moment of popularity and praise, he wept with compassion for what he saw, wishing with his whole heart that the people could be spared:

> If you, even you, had only recognized on this day the things that make for peace! But now they are hidden from your eyes. Indeed, the days will come upon you, when your enemies will set up ramparts around you and surround you, and hem you in on every side. They will crush you to the ground, you and your children within you, and they will not leave within you one stone upon another; because you did not recognize the time of your visitation from God. (Luke 19:42-44)

Christ never lost sight of the value of people or stopped having compassion for them—not even on the cross. Certainly it was compassion that moved him to ask God to forgive the soldiers who nailed him to the cross, "for they do not know what they are doing" (Luke 23:34). It was out of compassion that he promised paradise—as only he could—to a man who was dying the same death as he.

And so I am compelled to ask, How often is my teaching motivated by true compassion? When have I been perceptive enough to look past someone's material wealth and see their loneliness or their need for meaning in life? Do I look at people (my husband, children, parents, fellow Christians, difficult neighbors) and really love them before I speak truth that is hard to hear? Am I willing to take a good hard look at the person (made in the image of God) who is wasting away with AIDS, the battered woman who has run for her life, the divorced woman fighting for custody of her children, the pregnant teenager who feels she has no other option than abortion, the child sitting next to his dying mother in a refugee camp—or do I look away so I can sleep at night? Am I able to extend compassion even when I am hurting and feeling mistreated? How often do I weep over anything other than my own pain?

Not often enough. Compassion is not something that can be conjured up by a mere act of the will; it happens in us as we recognize that all people suffer. That is why compassion is revolutionary. When we begin to discover that the weaknesses, sins and sorrows of others are within us as well, we are changed in relation to them. It is hard to stay angry at someone when you realize that they hurt just as you do (whether they admit it or not), that they cry just as you do (whether they cry in front of you or not), that life is difficult for them just as it is for you (no matter how trouble free their life appears).

Yes, there is a time for anger, a time to say, "This is wrong and I must stand against it." But there is also a time (perhaps it is the same time) for compassion, for looking at the person on the other side of an argument, the person who has been cruel, the person who has all the power as well as the one who has very little, and seeing that their struggle with the human experience is our own. Their sin is the same sin to which we are prone. Cynicism melts away when hearts are laid bare and we look inside. And condescension seems totally out of place when we realize that "there but for the grace of God go I."

Henri Nouwen makes this observation:

> No one can help anyone without becoming involved, without entering with his whole person into the painful situation, without taking the risk of becoming hurt, wounded, or even destroyed in the process. Who can save a child from a burning house without taking the risk of being hurt by the flames? Who can listen to a story of loneliness without taking the risk of experiencing similar pains in his own heart and even losing his precious peace of mind? In short: who can take away suffering without entering it?

No one. Not even Christ himself.

CHRIST GAVE OF HIMSELF FREELY TO OTHERS

In the midst of rotting chicken pieces and dirty diapers, the poorest of the poor pick through the trash of Guatemala's city dump to find plastic containers to recycle, pieces of cardboard to shade them from the heat or morsels of food to keep them alive. The dump is their home, and they have little hope of ever leaving it. However, two women, Gladys Acuña and Lisbeth Piedrasanta, are there to offer them hope in Christ.

Gladys and Lisbeth left their comfortable counseling center and founded the Casa del Alfarero (Potter's House) fifty feet from the edge of the dump. With a team of thirty, they run a medical and dental clinic, offer carpentry and sewing classes, teach Bible lessons and serve up meals. Gladys serves as spiritual director and Lisbeth as administrative director. Their dream? In addition to meeting the physical needs of people who live in a place where fresh air is an impossibility and vultures fly overhead, they long to see spiritual revival. Says Lisbeth, "I ask the Lord not to let me die until I see spiritual revival here. We've been planting seeds for several years, and I would like to see kids seek the Lord sincerely. That is my desire: to see spiritual revival here, because I know that's the exit from their pain and suffering."

A life spent serving people who live in a dump? Somehow it seems like something Jesus would do.

Perhaps the most difficult aspect of Christ's life for us to emulate is his passion for serving others. That is why we are surprised when we find people like Lisbeth and Gladys actually doing it. Most of us are more like the disciples who, on the very night when Christ gave an example of servanthood by washing their feet, argued over who would have the most prominent positions in the kingdom. If we are at all honest, many of us would say that we too have wasted time and energy striving for positions of prominence at times when we could have been serving. How painful it is to realize that in those moments we are utterly unlike Christ.

The more I study the Scriptures, the clearer it becomes that love (not to be confused with dependency), humility (not to be confused with low self-esteem) and a servant's attitude (not to be equated with being a doormat) are the supreme Christian virtues. Christ modeled them perfectly. Conformity to Christ in these virtues must be top priority, *not because I am a woman but because I am a Christian.*

Answering the Call to Spiritual Transformation

One Sunday morning, Catherine Booth heard and accepted God's call to preach as her husband, William, a Methodist minister, finished his sermon. She later recalled her inner experience: "It seemed as if a voice said to me, 'Now if you were to go and testify, you know I

would bless it to your own soul as well as to the souls of the people.'
I gasped and said to my soul, . . . 'I cannot do it.' And then the devil
said, 'Besides, you are not prepared to speak. You will look like a fool
and have nothing to say.' "

Catherine chose to accept the Holy Spirit's challenge that day
rather than the doubts planted by Satan. She stood up in front of a
crowd of more than a thousand, packed into Bethesda Chapel, and
said, "I want to say a word." William was as surprised as anyone
when she made her sudden announcement, but he quickly recovered, and when she had finished, he announced that she would
preach that evening. Catherine's only regret was that she had waited
so long. She and William went on to found the Salvation Army.

Women today face the same choice as Catherine Booth did. Our
choice is not necessarily whether to preach or not to preach. It is how
to answer the challenge that the Holy Spirit is speaking to our soul,
whatever that is. For some it is the challenge to begin seeing ourselves as God sees us so we are more able to give of ourselves to others. For others, it is the challenge to pull our head out of their comfortable position in the sand and stand for what is right. For many in
affluent communities, the challenge is to get a grip on our materialism so we can invest in spiritual gain. For all of us, following in
Christ's footsteps will involve having a heart that breaks for the pain
of those who are still searching for love and meaning because they
have yet to find Christ. We too face the possibility of regret and the
question *Why did I wait so long?*

Soon after her pulpit debut, at least one of God's reasons in calling
Catherine Booth to preach became clear. William became ill. Because
his recovery was very slow, Catherine took over his entire preaching
circuit. Her dynamic and forceful speaking style drew crowds of
thousands. When William recovered, they were able to work to-

gether again in a revivalist ministry that involved preaching, rescue-mission work (especially with teenage prostitutes), founding the Salvation Army and training their own children in the ministry. Many agree that, as important as her work with the Salvation Army was, Catherine's thirty years of preaching ministry was perhaps most significant. "No man of her era exceeded her in popularity or spiritual results, including her husband."

I have heard the question asked, almost tongue-in-cheek, "Why should women be like Christ in humility and suffering yet unlike him in authority, power and exaltation?" The answer is: there is no reason at all. Catherine Booth is a flesh-and-blood example of what happens when a woman asks the question *How does Christ want to live his life uniquely through me?* and then follows him with freedom and abandon. Spiritual authority is born of her obedience, power is forged as she speaks the truth, and grace pours from her life as she channels her strength to serve others. The exaltation comes when we hear those words "Well done, good and faithful servant."

SPIRITUAL EXERCISES

Alone with God

Silence. As you come to the end of this chapter, take a few moments to sit with God in the silence of your heart. Allow yourself to simply sit with whatever desire has stirred in you through the reading of this chapter.

- As you read this chapter, what aspect of the life of Christ stirred you most deeply?

- Allow yourself to imagine observing Christ in that particular expression of his character. What do you see? What do you feel?

  Prayer and journaling. Review what you have just read, noticing the places of resonance and resistance that you have highlighted. Notice the places where you say, "I really want that" and "I'm not sure I'm up for that!" What is the one aspect of the life of Christ that you feel called to live into more fully at this time? Tell God what's true about you right now and what you long for. Then listen for his response.

Invitations. God, how are you inviting me to respond to what I've read today?

A Look at 1 Timothy 2:11-12 and God's View of Women

As chapter three suggests, 1 Timothy 2:11-12 offers an opportunity to wrestle with a complex Scripture passage. Addressing the church in Ephesus, Paul wrote, "Let a woman learn in silence with full submission. I permit no woman to teach or to have authority over a man; she is to keep silent." This is the primary passage from which people infer that the scope of women's ministry is to be limited. While an exhaustive study of this passage and related research is beyond the scope of this book, I would like to provide an overview of important research that sheds greater light on these difficult verses.

HISTORICAL CONTEXT

At the time Paul wrote this letter to believers, Ephesus stood as a bastion of feminine supremacy in religion. The shrine of the great mother goddess Artemis (or Diana, as the Romans knew her) was located in Ephesus, and there she was worshiped as the mother of gods and men. It was believed that she was the originator of life and that her presence or intervention guaranteed economic and political security.

It was in this religious climate that Gnosticism, with its radical distortions of biblical stories, began to develop and infiltrate the church. One such distortion twisted the story of Eve to say that she was the one who brought life to Adam. Richard Kroeger and Catherine Clark Kroeger write: "According to gnostic thought, all matter was evil. The Creator, the God of the Hebrew Bible, was evil because he made the material world. The serpent was beneficent in helping Adam and Eve to shake off the deception perpetrated on them by the Creator, and Eve was the mediator who brought true knowledge to the human race."

The veneration of Eve that grew out of this Gnostic distortion dovetailed perfectly with the practice of goddess worship that was already firmly entrenched in the religious psyche of Ephesians in the first century. It was a logical progression to mythologize and deify Eve as the mediator of truth and special hidden knowledge. Gnostics developed an entire belief system that claimed that mystic knowledge resided not only in feminine figures of sacred literature (such as Eve and Mary the mother of Jesus) but also in living Gnostic women who were willing to share their divine secrets. These secrets were often conveyed through repetitive syllables, riddles and paradoxes that apparently made sense to Gnostics themselves but were very difficult for anyone else to understand and refute.

Paul wrote to his young protégé Timothy for the express purpose of encouraging him to stay at the church in Ephesus to combat such false teaching: "I urge you . . . to remain in Ephesus so that you may instruct certain people not to teach any different doctrine, and not to occupy themselves with myths and endless genealogies that promote speculations rather than divine training that is known by faith" (1 Timothy 1:3-4). The church in Ephesus was not a healthy church; it was in crisis due in part to confusion about the woman's role as mediator of religious truth. Harsher-than-normal rules were needed to give these women an opportunity to learn from and submit themselves to the true mediator of knowledge—Jesus Christ, as revealed in the Scriptures and the teaching of the apostles.

KEYWORDS

It is important that we understand the meaning of two keywords in Greek: *hesychia* (translated "silent" in many versions of 1 Timothy 2:11-12) and *authentein* (translated "to have authority" in verse 12).

According to widely respected Greek scholar W. E. Vine, *hesychia* denotes "quietness" or "tranquility arising from within."[2] He does not even list "silence" as a possible translation. Consistent with this definition, *hesychia* is translated "quiet" in 2 Thessalonians 3:12, "Such persons we command and exhort in the Lord Jesus Christ to do their work quietly [*hesychia*]," and 1 Timothy 2:2, "so that we may lead a quiet [*hesychia*, adjective form] and peaceable life."

There is a world of difference between the absolute silence implied by the translations to which most of us have had access and the quiet tranquillity that a more careful translation describes! We need to ask ourselves, why would the translators make this kind of word choice? What impact does a more accurate translation have on our understanding of the role of women?

The word *authentein* presents us with a different kind of challenge. There are several other Greek words translated "authority" in the New Testament, and this is the only time *authentein* appears there. In cases like this, it is common practice for translators to turn to secular literature of the same period for clues as to the meaning of such a rare word. However, in the case of the word *authentein,* it is not that easy. Until the twentieth century, it was not found in any other works written around Paul's time! With this keyword being so difficult to pin down, no wonder scholars have found the passage hard to understand.

Fortunately, recent scholarship has uncovered new information about this rarely used word. The Kroegers, who are Greek scholars, offer a fascinating study of *authentein* based on their extensive research of ancient history and literature. By tracing this word through ancient documents, they have found that it had a wide range of meanings, as follows:

1. to begin something, to be primarily responsible for a condition or action (especially murder)
2. to rule, to dominate
3. to usurp power or rights from another
4. to claim ownership, sovereignty or authorship

Furthermore, new sources in classical Greek literature demonstrate that *authentein* was often used to refer to religious activity that was characterized by promiscuity, reversal of gender roles, sex and death mingled together, murder and women claiming a monopoly on religious power (as among the Amazons). In addition, the Kroegers found several older dictionaries in which *authentein is* defined "to represent oneself as the author, originator, or source of something." This definition is particularly interesting in light of the fact that in the ancient world of Asia Minor, many viewed women as the ultimate source of life. These meanings put a whole new spin on 1 Timothy 2:12 as we consider how a more careful translation might clarify Paul's meaning.

Again, why would Paul, a scholarly writer, use such a rare word that carried with it such unpleasant connotations? If he meant to bar women from all legitimate authority, he could have used any of several other words that are much more straightforward in meaning.

GRAMMATICAL STRUCTURE

The grammatical structure of verse 12 is noteworthy. It contains three infinitives: to teach, *authentein* and to be. The Kroegers suggest that the separation of "to teach" from the other infinitives (apparent in any Greek New Testament or interlinear) may indicate that one or more of these two infinitives deal with the content of a woman's teaching. They point out that Paul never used the infinitive "to teach" without accompanying clarification as to the content of the teaching. In Paul's writings, the infinitive "to teach" is always accompanied by another verb that serves to sharpen its focus. For instance, in 1 Timothy 1:3-4 Paul says, "Instruct certain people not to teach any different doctrine, and not to occupy themselves with myths and endless genealogies." And in 1 Timothy 6:3 he speaks of one who "teaches otherwise and does not agree with the sound words of our Lord Jesus Christ." The verb "to teach" *(didaskein),* linked as it is to the verb *authentein* by the negative *oude* (meaning "nor"), gives us the possibility that *authentein* serves to explain what *kind* of teaching is prohibited to women. An alternate translation would then be "I do not permit a woman to teach nor represent herself as originator (or source) of man, but she is to be peaceable."

CULTURE AND TRANSLATION

As you can see, translation is a complex process that is rife with challenges. When we translate the inspired Word of God from the original language, we face the difficulty of word equivalency and cultural considerations. Translators often have a range of English words to choose from when translating particular Greek words into English. The final word choice is left to their discretion. Further, in Greek sentence structure, the words are not in the order to which we are accustomed. This requires that the translators (again, at their discretion) arrange the words in an order that makes sense to the English reader. This is a process that is subjective, at best, and yet the order of words can have a significant impact on meaning.

It is difficult for a translator to maintain objectivity; the temptation always exists to translate a passage to be consistent with the way one already sees life. When we consider that most translators have been men from societies that did not appropriately value women and some of their gifts, it is not difficult to see how some of the more obscure words and passages could be translated with a bias. That's why it is important for us as women to become students of the Scriptures ourselves rather than merely taking other people's word for it. Then we can do our own hard work of discovering what God is saying to us through his Word.

FURTHER READING

If you want to explore these biblical and theological questions further, here's a list of key books.

Bilezikian, Gilbert. *Beyond Sex Roles: What the Bible Says About a Woman's Place in Church and Family.* 3rd ed. Grand Rapids: Baker, 2006.

Kroeger, Richard, and Catherine Clark. *I Suffer Not a Woman: Rethinking I Timothy 2:11-15 in Light of Ancient Evidence.* Grand Rapids: Baker, 1992.

Pierce, Ronald W., and Rebecca Merrill Groothuis. *Discovering Biblical Equality: Complementarity Without Hierarchy.* Downers Grove, Ill.: InterVarsity Press, 2005.

Tucker, Ruth, and Walter Liefeld. *Daughters of the Church.* Grand Rapids: Zondervan, 1987.

Van Leeuwen, Mary Stewart. *Gender and Grace: Love, Work & Parenting in a Changing World.* Downers Grove, Ill.: InterVarsity Press, 1990.

APPENDIX B

Guide for Discussion
with a Spiritual Friend

In addition to thinking through the spiritual exercises found at the
end of each chapter, or in their place, you may want to follow a more
structured approach to working through this book. The guide below
offers questions that can be used with a spiritual friend one-on-one
or in a small group. They can also be used for individual reflection
and journaling.

INTRODUCTION: AN INVITATION TO TRANSFORMATION IN CHRIST

Silence. Begin your time together with a moment of silence and a simple prayer of invitation for God to join you. Remember that this time
is not meant for solving problems, giving advice or catching up on
each other's work or family life. This is a time to pay attention to the
invitations of God in each other's life, to support one another through
listening and loving, and to pray that God will enable each of you to
respond faithfully to the calling to spiritual transformation.

Listening. Take turns giving each other undivided attention. Give
each other a brief summary of what has happened between you and
God this week in the context of your spiritual practices and your
reading of this chapter.

- What did God say to you in your times of solitude and silence?

- What were your experiences of resonance and resistance as you read this chapter? How did you process those with God in your journal?

- What is the choice point that you are facing right now?

- Was there anything in your reading and reflection that seemed to offer guidance for you?

- Does God seem to be inviting you to do anything as a result of where you have been with him this week?

Prayer. At the end of your time together, ask, "How would you like me to pray for you?" Then take time to pray for one another. It is much easier to talk about prayer than to actually do it, so try to be disciplined about including prayer in your spiritual companionship.

CHAPTER 1: FINDING OUR IDENTITY IN CHRIST

Silence. Begin your time together with a moment of silence and a simple prayer of invitation for God to join you.

Listening. Take turns giving each other undivided attention. Give each other a brief summary of what has happened between you and God this week in the context of your spiritual practices and your reading of this chapter.

- What did God say to you in your times of solitude and silence?

- What were your experiences of resonance and resistance as you read this chapter? How did you process those with God in your journal?

- In what area of self-esteem do you experience yourself as being weak and deficient or strong and confident?

- How do you notice yourself looking to others to fill any gaps in your self-esteem?

- Is there anything in your reading and reflection that offers you guidance about how to allow Christ to become all that you need in this area?

- Does God seem to be inviting you to do anything as a result of where you have been with him this week?

Prayer. Ask, "How would you like me to pray for you?" and take time to pray for one another.

Chapter 2: Saying Yes to God's Purposes

Silence. Begin your time together with a moment of silence and a simple prayer of invitation for God to join you.

Listening. Take turns giving each other undivided attention. Give each other a brief summary of what has happened between you and God this week in the context of your spiritual practices and your reading of this chapter.

- What did God say to you in your times of solitude and silence about the package that he is putting together in your life?

- What were your experiences of resonance and resistance as you read this chapter? How did you process those with God in your journal?

- What element of purposeful living is missing from your life right now?

- How is God inviting you to a deeper level of freedom in saying yes to his purposes?

- Does God seem to be inviting you to do anything as a result of where you have been with him this week?

Prayer. Pray for one another.

CHAPTER 3: SERVING GOD IN THE WAY THAT HE CALLS

Silence. Begin your time together with a moment of silence and a simple prayer of invitation for God to join you.

Listening. Take turns giving each other undivided attention. Give each other a brief summary of what has happened between you and God this week in the context of your spiritual practices and your reading of this chapter.

- What did God say to you in your times of solitude and silence?
- What were your experiences of resonance and resistance as you read this chapter? How did you process those with God in your journal?
- What memories did this chapter trigger in you about yourself as a little girl learning what it meant to be a woman?
- What were the strongest messages you received?
- Which of these messages do you agree with or disagree with now that you are a grown woman looking to God for your truest identity?
- What questions do you still have?
- How does God seem to be inviting you to process those questions with him?

Prayer. Pray for one another.

CHAPTER 4: LIVING IN TRUTH

Silence. Begin your time together with a moment of silence and a simple prayer of invitation for God to join you.

Listening. Take turns giving each other undivided attention. Give each other a brief summary of what has happened between you and God this week in the context of your spiritual practices and your reading of this chapter.

- What did God say to you in your times of solitude and silence?

- What were your experiences of resonance and resistance as you read this chapter? How did you process those with God in your journal?

- What is the area of your life where God is speaking to you about the need to walk in truth?

- What is it like for you to consider telling more truth or living into more truth in this area?

- What kind of support do you need?

  Prayer. Pray for one another.

CHAPTER 5: ESCAPING THE TYRANNY OF THE "NEVER-ENOUGH" WORLD

Silence. Begin your time together with a moment of silence and a simple prayer of invitation for God to join you.

Listening. Take turns giving each other undivided attention. Give each other a brief summary of what has happened between you and God this week in the context of your spiritual practices and your reading of this chapter.

- What did God say to you in your times of solitude and silence?

- What were your experiences of resonance and resistance as you read this chapter? How did you process those with God in your journal?

- To what dangers of the material world are you most vulnerable right now?

- What empty places in your soul do you try to fill with something from the material world?

- How is God inviting you to fill those empty places with something that is truly satisfying? (Try to be as concrete as possible.)

Prayer. Pray for one another.

CHAPTER 6: CULTIVATING A MARRIAGE THAT WORKS

Silence. Begin your time together with a moment of silence and a simple prayer of invitation for God to join you.

Listening. Take turns giving each other undivided attention. Give each other a brief summary of what has happened between you and God this week in the context of your spiritual practices and your reading of this chapter.

- What did God say to you in your times of solitude and silence?

- As you read about fears, hopes, ideals and ambivalence about marriage in this chapter, which emotions and concepts resonated with you? Which ones did you find yourself resisting?

- What questions do you want to bring to God about your thoughts and emotions toward marriage?

- If you are married, how do you work with the issues of headship and submission in your marriage?

- In what areas of your marriage do you feel freedom and joy?

- In what areas of your marriage do you feel sad or stuck?

- How is God changing you in the midst of the joys and pain of living so intimately with another human being? What are his invitations to you?

Prayer. Pray for one another.

CHAPTER 7: EMBRACING OUR SEXUALITY

Silence. Begin your time together with a moment of silence and a simple prayer of invitation for God to join you.

Listening. Take turns giving each other undivided attention. As appropriate, give each other a brief summary of what has happened between you and God this week in the context of your spiritual practices and your reading of this chapter.

- What did God say to you in your times of solitude and silence?

- What were your experiences of resonance and resistance as you read this chapter? How did you process those with God in your journal? In this area in particular, share only what you feel comfortable sharing.

- If you feel comfortable doing so, talk about one or more of the following questions:

  1. How are you experiencing your sexuality these days—as a gift, as a burden, as a complication?

  2. Do you experience your sexuality as being at all connected with your spirituality?

  3. Is there any piece of information or perspective offered in this chapter that you think will help you experience greater freedom in living before God as a sexual being?

Prayer. Pray for one another.

CHAPTER 8: EXPERIENCING THE TRANSFORMATION OF MOTHERHOOD

Silence. Begin your time together with a moment of silence and a simle prayer of invitation for God to join you.

Listening. Take turns giving each other undivided attention. As appropriate, tell each other some of what has happened between you and God this week in the context of your spiritual practices and your reading of this chapter.

- What did God say to you in your times of solitude and silence?

- What were your experiences of resonance and resistance as you read this chapter? How did you process those with God in your journal?

- How is God transforming you in the midst of your mothering?

- What is the area of your deepest joy as a mother these days?

- What is your deepest question or concern?

- When you ask God, "What will it require of me to nurture the emotional, physical and spiritual well-being of my children?" what do you hear?

Prayer. Pray for one another.

CHAPTER 9: FINDING GOD IN THE MIDST OF DIFFICULTY

Silence. Begin your time together with a moment of silence and a simple prayer of invitation for God to join you.

Listening. Take turns giving each other undivided attention. In this area in particular, share only that which you feel comfortable sharing. As appropriate, specify the area of your life that this chapter seems to speak to. Give each other a brief summary of what has happened between you and God this week in the context of your spiritual practices and your reading of this chapter.

- What did God say to you in your times of solitude and silence?

- What were your experiences of resonance and resistance as you read this chapter? How did you process those with God in your journal?

- How is God meeting you in the midst of your difficulty?

- This chapter mentions several ways in which we can allow the beauty of Christ to emerge in us—being honest with God, letting difficulties produce character, allowing difficulties to bond us with others, allowing God to use our weaknesses. Which of these invitations to spiritual transformation seem to be God's invitation to you at this time?

Prayer. Pray for one another.

CHAPTER 10: REACHING ACROSS GENERATIONS

Silence. Begin your time together with a moment of silence and a simple prayer of invitation for God to join you.

Listening. Take turns giving each other undivided attention. Give each other a brief summary of what has happened between you and God this week in the context of your spiritual practices and your reading of this chapter.

- What did God say to you in your times of solitude and silence?

- What were your experiences of resonance and resistance as you read this chapter? How did you process those with God in your journal?

- Who are the older women God seems to be using to provide some light for your journey into spiritual transformation?

- Who are the younger women who seem to be looking to you for light?

- Are there any next steps that God is inviting you to take in any of these relationships?

Prayer. Pray for one another.

CHAPTER 11: BEING CHRIST IN THE WORLD

Silence. Begin your time together with a moment of silence and a simple prayer of invitation for God to join you.

Listening. Take turns giving each other undivided attention. Give each other a brief summary of what has happened between you and God this week in the context of your spiritual practices and your reading of this chapter.

• What did God say to you in your times of solitude and silence?

• What were your experiences of resonance and resistance as you read this chapter? How did you process those with God in your journal?

• How do you feel about the possibility of being a unique expression of Christ's life in this world?

• As you observe Christ's way of being in the world, what stirs in your heart in terms of your desire to be transformed into his likeness? What is your intent?

Prayer. At the end of your time together, take time to pray for one another. In preparation for this time of prayer, you might want to review the themes of this book and identify those things that stand out as God's clearest invitations to each of you. Then pray that God would continue to enable each of you to respond faithfully to his invitations to truth, freedom and spiritual transformation.

N O T E S

Introduction: A Invitation to Transformation in Christ

p. 13   "In general, feminism gave men": "The Failures of Feminism," November 19, 1990, p. 9.

p. 13   The Fortune 500 vice president is quoted in Jaclyn Fierman, "Why Women Still Don't Hit the Top," *Fortune,* July 30, 1990, p. 58.

pp. 13-14   "a state of flux": Peggy Orenstein, *Flux: Women on Sex, Work, Love, Kids and Life in a Half-Changed World* (New York: Anchor, 2000), quote from pp. 4, 17.

pp. 18-21   Material on silence and solitude adapted from Ruth Haley Barton, *Invitation to Solitude & Silence* (Downers Grove, Ill.: InterVarsity Press, 2004).

Chapter 1: Finding Our Identity in Christ

pp. 24-25   "I want first of all": Anne Morrow Lindbergh, *Gift from the Sea,* rev. ed. (New York: Pantheon, 1975), pp. 16-17.

p. 25   "Woman's recurring lesson": Ibid., p. 128.

p. 26   "Studies of women have repeatedly shown": Caryl Rivers, Rosalind Barnett and Grace Baruch, *Beyond Sugar and Spice: How Women Grow, Learn and Thrive* (New York: Putnam, 1979), p. 25.

p. 26   ". . . her experience in the family": See for example, Linda Tschirhart Sanford and Mary Ellen Donovan, *Women and Self-Esteem* (New York: Penguin, 1984), p. 40.

p. 28   "There is still no country": Emily MacFarquhar, "The War Against Women," *U.S. News & World Report,* March 28, 1994, p. 44. Further facts from this article (pp. 44-56):

- In the new Russia, women applying for office jobs are often told that their duties include sleeping with the boss. A typical want ad reads, "Not older than 25; bright appearance, long legs compulsory."
- In China, India, and other nations where sons are still valued more highly than daughters, ultrasound is now being used to determine the sex of babies so that females can be aborted or poison can be administered at birth.
- In some Islamic countries, rape *victims* are charged and imprisoned for adul-

tery. Those who try to fight such inequities receive death threats, have their passports revoked and their writings banned.

- In parts of Africa, the Middle East and Asia, genital mutilation, the traditional removing of all or part of a girl's outer genitalia, is still practiced. Female circumcision (removal of the hood of the clitoris), clitoridectomy (removal of the clitoris) and genital infibulation (removal of the clitoris and labia and stitching the vulva together, leaving only a small opening for urine and menstrual flow) are procedures performed without anesthesia, causing severe medical problems and removing almost any possibility for sexual pleasure.

- In India, bride burnings, dowry murders and "stove burstings" ("domestic accidents" in which a young wife is killed) are common forms of domestic violence that take the lives of many women whose families cannot keep paying for their protection. In countries where dowries can add up to ten times a man's annual income, dowry extortion is very common, and there is little protection for the women who are being used as merchandise.

- In industrial nations, women's pay still averages two-thirds that of men, mainly because women are clustered in low-wage "women's jobs." In the United States, for instance, year-round full-time working women earned 71 percent of the male wage in 1992, and women high school graduates earned slightly less than did men who dropped out of school before ninth grade.

p. 31   "I was beginning to listen": Kari Torjesen Malcolm, *Women at the Crossroads* (Downers Grove, Ill.: InterVarsity Press, 1982), pp. 40-41.

p. 32   Samara was also of a lesser race: In Jewish culture women were viewed as little more than the "property" of fathers or husbands. In addition, Jews viewed Samaritans as "leftovers" from Israel because their ancestors had intermarried with foreigners after the chiefs and nobles had been captured during the Babylonian captivity. "Real Jews" despised Samaritans because they felt that the Samaritans had sold their birthright. Consequently, they had forced the Samaritans to build their own place of worship at Mount Gerazim. Most Jews avoided contact with Samaritans at all costs, choosing to go around Samaria rather than through it.

pp. 32-33   He revealed new truth to Samara: Jesus told her that God was abolishing the old way of worshiping, which was based on outward rituals. In its place, he was ushering in a new kind of worship that was not associated with any outward trappings but involved the spirit of the worshiper (John 4:23). This would be a radical shift!

p. 33   "Many women we interviewed": Linda Tschirhart Sanford and Mary Ellen Donovan, *Women and Self-Esteem* (New York: Penguin, 1984), p. 12.

pp. 34-35   Mary Stewart Van Leeuwen draws our attention: Mary Stewart Van Leeuwen, *Gender and Grace* (Downers Grove, Ill.: InterVarsity Press, 1990), p. 46.

p. 38   "We have been made": Lawrence J. Crabb, *Understanding People* (Grand Rapids: Zondervan, 1987), p. 110.

p. 41   We women also need to understand: For an excellent review of practical information women need to have, see Florence Littauer, *Wake Up, Women! Submission Doesn't Mean Stupidity* (Dallas: Word, 1994).

p. 43   "I am complete in Christ" and the affirmations that follow are from Marie Chapian, *Staying Happy in an Unhappy World* (Old Tappan, N.J.: Revell, 1985), p. 37.

Chapter 2: Saying Yes to God's Purposes

p. 48   "Life without meaning is the torture of restlessness": Edgar Lee Masters, "George Grey," in *Spoon River Anthology* (1915; reprint, New York: Penguin, 1992).

p. 49   At the end of this seven-day banquet: Regarding Xerxes' request of Vashti, one commentator notes, "Had the king been sober, he would not have considered such a breach of custom, for he knew that Eastern women lived in seclusion and that such a request as he made in this drunken condition amounted to a gross insult. For Vashti to appear in the banquet hall, though dressed in her royal robes and crowned, would be almost as degrading as for a modern woman to go naked into a man's party. What Xerxes demanded was a surrender of womanly honor, and Vashti, who was neither vain nor wanton, was unwilling to comply." Herbert Lockyer, *All the Women of the Bible* (Grand Rapids: Zondervan, 1958), pp. 165-66.

p. 56   "Discovering Vocation": Parker Palmer, *Let Your Life Speak: Listening for the Voice of Vocation* (San Francisco: Jossey-Bass Publishers, 2000), p.19.

p. 59   "Only those who turn down": Miriam Adeney, *A Time for Risking* (Portland, Ore.: Multnomah Press, 1987), pp. 61 and 56-57.

p. 60   One way to become more intentional: For a step-by-step workbook on purposeful living, see Ruth Haley Barton, *Becoming Women of Purpose,* rev. ed. (Colorado Springs: Shaw, 2001).

Chapter 3: Serving God in the Way That He Calls

p. 67   One woman said, "I have read the Bible": This is quoted in Linda Tschirhart Sanford and Mary Ellen Donovan, *Women and Self-Esteem* (New York: Penguin, 1984), p. 173.

p. 67   My heart was stirred: You can read about Abigail, Deborah, Huldah, Esther and Priscilla in 1 Samuel 25; Judges 4–5; 2 Kings 22:14-20, the book of Esther and Acts 18:24-26 respectively.

p. 67   After I finished writing: That first Bible study is now published as *Women Like Us: Wisdom for Today's Issues,* rev. ed. (Colorado Springs: Shaw, 2001).

p. 69   "The one who helps": Ruth A. Tucker, *Women in the Maze* (Downers Grove, Ill.: InterVarsity Press, 1992), pp. 37-38.

p. 74   "More than a hundred passages in the Bible": L. E. Maxwell, quoted in Richard Kroeger and Catherine Clark Kroeger, *I Suffer Not a Woman* (Grand Rapids: Baker, 1992), p. 33.

p. 75   But now Paul is saying: The Kroegers note that the phrase "silence and submission" is a Near Eastern formula implying willingness to heed and obey instruction—in this case that instruction contained in the Word of God. Indeed, the rabbinic scholar himself was required to learn in silence, as this was how one gained knowledge of God (ibid., pp. 75-76).

Chapter 4: Living in Truth

p. 82   She was determined: In Bible times, the blessing from father to son was like an oral will that was legally binding and could not be revoked. Each child usually received a blessing, but the oldest son got a special one that included prosperity, leadership of the family and divine judgment on those who opposed him. In the case of Esau, his father's blessing would also have included the privilege of having God's promise to Abraham fulfilled through him: "I will make you the father of a multitude of nations" (Genesis 17:4-5 NASB).

pp. 83-84   As far as we know: It is assumed that Rebekah died during Jacob's long absence and was buried in the cave of Machpelah near Hebron (Genesis 49:31). Herbert Lockyer, *All the Women of the Bible* (Grand Rapids: Zondervan, 1958), p. 140.

p. 84   "Pretending reflects deep prohibitions": Harriet Goldhor Lerner, *The Dance of Deception* (New York: HarperCollins, 1993), p. 14.

p. 90   "Once something is defined as unfeminine: Ibid., p. 49.

p. 90   "Females in our culture are reinforced": Carolyn Stahl Bohler, *When You Need to Take a Stand* (Louisville, Ky.: Westminster John Knox, 1990), p. 63.

p. 91   "The word *integrity* comes from the Latin": William Backus, *Telling Each Other the Truth* (Minneapolis: Bethany House, 1985), p. 26.

p. 91   "Tunnel of chaos . . . where hurts are unburied": Bill Hybels, *Honest to God?* (Grand Rapids: Zondervan, 1990), p. 56.

p. 92   "Our customs of speech frequently skirt the truth": Backus, *Telling Each Other the Truth*, pp. 16-17.

p. 96   We are trying all the time to extend the possibilities of truth: This concept is from Lerner, *Dance of Deception*, p. 218.

Chapter 5: Escaping the Tyranny of the "Never-Enough" World

p. 100   In the never-enough world: Materialism is the theory that physical well-being and worldly possessions constitute life's greatest good and highest value.

p. 101   "Consume, consume, consume": Vance Packard, *The Hidden Persuaders* (New York: Simon & Schuster, 1957), p. 14.

p. 102   "Once these points of vulnerability": Ibid., p. 30.

p. 102   "What makes this country great": Quoted in ibid., p. 16.

p. 103   "For most of human history": Landon Y. Jones, "The Baby Boomers," *Money*, March 1983, p. 300.

p. 104   "He liked the good life of Sodom's society": Allen P. Ross, "Genesis," in *The Bible Knowledge Commentary*, ed. John F. Walvoord and Roy Zuck (Wheaton, Ill.: Victor, 1985), p. 60.

pp. 105-6   "Credit ruined my marriage" and "The most awful thing to deal with": this story is from Mike Starkey, *Born to Shop* (Eastbourne, U.K.: Monarch, 1989), pp. 106-7.

Chapter 6: Cultivating a Marriage That Works

p. 115   "I became a submissive wife": Slaikeu Lawhead, *The Lie of the Good Life* (Portland, Ore.: Multnomah Press, 1989), pp. 70-71.

pp. 115-16   "While it may seem easiest": James H. Olthuis, *I Pledge You My Troth* (San Francisco: Harper & Row, 1975), pp. 36-37.

p. 118   "The word *head* is virtually synonymous": *Theological Dictionary of the New Testament*, ed. Gerhard Kittel (Grand Rapids: Eerdman's, 1965), 3:673-82.

p. 118   "The concept of headship in the New Testament": Gilbert Bilezikian, *Beyond Sex Roles* (Grand Rapids: Baker, 1985), p. 161.

p. 124   Much of the tiredness and "trappedness": Jeff Van Vonderen, *Families Where Grace Is in Place* (Minneapolis: Bethany House, 1992).

p. 126   Data from interviews of divorced male CEOs comes from Julie Connelly, "The CEO's Second Wife," *Fortune*, August 28, 1989, p. 55.

pp. 127-28   "Although many things were strong in my marriage": Quoted in Lawhead, *Lie of the Good Life*, pp. 126-27.

Chapter 7: Embracing Our Sexuality

p. 132   Feelings of shame about sexuality: Robert Crooks and Karla Bauer explore the prevalence and effects of sexual abuse in *Our Sexuality* (Redwood City, Calif.: Benjamin-Cummings, 1993). Only recently has society begun to lift the shroud of silence that has obscured this painful issue. More and more victims of this abuse of power are finally beginning to speak about their suffering and to grapple with the long-range effect it has had on their lives.

> There is increasing evidence that child sexual abuse can be a severely traumatizing and emotionally damaging experience with long-term negative consequences for the victim. Clinical contact with adult survivors of child sexual abuses often reveals memories of a joyless youth filled with pain. Survivors speak of their loss of childhood innocence, the contamination and interruption of normal sexual development, and a profound sense of betrayal at the hands of a beloved family [member] or trusted friend. . . . Many victims have difficulty forming intimate adult relationships, particularly with men. When relationships with men are established, they are frequently devoid of emotional and sexual fulfillment. Sexual abuse is not uncommon in the histories of women who seek treatment for sexual difficulties. (p. 656)

Although there are no simple solutions to the pain of sexual abuse, a sexual abuse survivor owes it to herself and to those she loves to deal with this difficult part of her past. Karen, a survivor of child sexual abuse and rape, has this to say:

> Healing is painfully slow and difficult. Both therapists I have worked with have suggested a seven-to-ten-year recovery process. I have struggled to overcome guilt and shame, finally being able to admit I did not invite the experiences of childhood abuse or rape. I am still working on remembering parts of my story. I continue to express anger and rage, which are essential to my healing. I have learned to trust some people. And I still grieve for the losses. . . . I can now cry in a limited fashion, and my self-concept and self-esteem are fairly restored.

> Incest and rape are not about sex. They are about power and control. It's about big people over little people, superior over subordinate. To heal re-

quires that I gain a sense of control over my life. I've gained enough control to make the transition from victim to survivor. The healing process is long, but I've surrendered to the fact that being in the process of healing is a respectable and legitimate place to be. I deserve to heal. My greatest victory is to break the promise [not to tell] and tell my story. I have been able to use the power of writing and speech to transform, to change anger, fear, shame and guilt into useful tools for cutting away lies and deception (quoted in James Newton Poling, *The Abuse of Power* [Nashville: Abingdon, 1991], p. 41).

pp. 137-38   Nicolette's story: Slaikeu Lawhead, *The Lie of the Good Life* (Portland, Ore.: Multnomah Press, 1989), pp. 114-15.

p. 38   Ann (not her real name) is a friend of mine.

Freud was convinced that every woman wished she had a penis and that that was exactly what the clitoris is—a stunted penis. This led him to conclude that erotic sensations, arousal and orgasm resulting from direct stimulation of the clitoris were all expressions of "masculine" rather than "feminine" sexuality—and therefore were undesirable. At adolescence a woman was supposed to transfer her erotic center from the clitoris to the vagina. If she was not able to do so at this time, psychotherapy was sometimes used to help her attain "vaginal" orgasms. Unfortunately, this theory led many women to believe incorrectly that they were sexually maladjusted. Today we understand that Freud's theory was physiologically inaccurate (Crooks and Bauer, *Our Sexuality*, pp. 171-72).

p. 141   "The natural noises and behaviors": Clifford Penner and Joyce Penner, *The Gift of Sex* (Waco, Tex.: Word, 1981), pp. 304-5.

p. 142   "Men are the initiators": See also ibid.

p. 145   "Sexuality mimics love": Elizabeth Haich, quoted in Gabrielle Brown, *Why More Men and Women Are Abstaining from Sex—and Enjoying It* (New York: McGraw-Hill, 1980), p. 212.

p. 146   "The greatest sexual ecstasy: Quoted in Dana Kennedy, "The New Monogamy," *Daily Herald* (Chicago), February 18, 1993, sec. 8, p. 1.

p. 148   "Swimming in warm water": Quoted in Linda Tschirhart Sanford and Mary Ellen Donovan, *Women and Self-Esteem* (New York: Penguin, 1984), p. 401.

p. 148   From 60 to 80 percent of women masturbate: This figure is from Crooks and Bauer, *Our Sexuality.*

p. 148   There is ample evidence: David F. Hurlbert and Karen E. Whittaker, "The Role of Masturbation in Marital and Sexual Satisfaction: A Comparative Study of Female Masturbators and Nonmasturbators," *Journal of Sex Education and Therapy* 17 (1991): 272-82.

Therapy programs for the married woman who has not yet learned to experience orgasm are based on progressive self-awareness activities such as body exploration, self-examination of the genitals, self-stimulation to learn about pleasure and arousal, and self-stimulation to orgasm. Once a woman has experienced orgasm through self-stimulation, she progresses step by step toward experiencing orgasm with her husband by guiding him as he stimulates her. They can then incorporate what they have learned into their experiences with sexual intercourse. This process takes time and commitment but can greatly enhance a woman's ability to respond to her husband. Her willingness to take responsibility for learning about herself, for pursuing the pleasure of orgasm and sharing what she has learned with her husband, is one of the keys to her sexual fulfillment.

p. 149   Unmarried adults often suffer: The "evils" of masturbation received a great deal of publicity in the name of science during the 1800s and early 1900s, when certain physicians attributed such maladies as blindness, stupidity, tuberculosis, insanity and idiocy to this practice (Crooks and Bauer, *Our Sexuality*, p. 252).

In addition, strongly negative attitudes toward masturbation have been based on the belief, from one stream of the Judeo-Christian tradition, that procreation is the only legitimate purpose for sexual activity. Because masturbation does not result in pregnancy, it has often been condemned. This, added to the sexual/ spiritual split discussed earlier, has made it easy for religious folks to look askance at this way of enjoying one's own body.

For a complete discussion of biblical guidelines around masturbation see Penner and Penner, *Gift of Sex*, p. 231.

p. 151   Ann Birk and her story: Caryl Rivers, Rosalind Barnett and Grace Baruch, *Beyond Sugar and Spice: How Women Grow, Learn and Thrive* (New York: Putnam, 1979), p. 207.

p. 152   Psychiatrist M. Scott Peck: M. Scott Peck, *Further Along the Road Less Traveled* (New York Simon & Schuster, 1993), p. 225.

p. 153   "Many think that sexuality": Alice Peterson's words are from a personal interview with me, and she has given me permission to quote them.

Chapter 8: Experiencing the Transformations of Motherhood

pp. 161-62   "To welcome a child": Wendy Wright, *Sacred Dwelling: A Spirituality of Family Life* (Leavenworth, Kans.: Forest of Peace, 1994), p. 31.

p. 166   "One can never wrestle enough with God": Simone Weil, *Waiting for God* (New York: Perennial Classics, 2001), p. 27.

p. 172   Bill Hybels wisely encourages: *Honest to God?* (Grand Rapids: Zondervan, 1992), pp. 85-88.

p. 173   Just as the men and women of Israel: In Jewish culture, the raising of children was a real family affair. Education of the children was the mother's responsibility for the first three years (probably until weaning), but after that, religious education of the sons became the father's responsibility. During this time he also taught them the family trade. In addition, extended families lived together, so that grandparents, aunts, uncles and older children participated in caring for the younger ones.

p. 173   Raising children is not "women's work": A greater sharing in the joys, frustrations and hard work of parenting will benefit not only women but men and their children as well. Mary Stewart Van Leeuwen details the benefits to children at great length in a chapter on coparenting in her book *Gender & Grace*. For example, she cites a study in which psychologist Michael Yogman found that men and women tend to play with their children in different ways. Fathers were more likely to engage in physical play, tapping or patting younger infants and doing controlled roughhousing with older ones. Mothers made more sounds and played more verbal games with their children, particularly games involving imitation and taking turns. Yogman's conclusion is that "children need both kinds of play for social and intellectual development. The mother-infant dialogues encourage language development and turn-taking, while the father's more physically oriented games help develop spatial and motor skills" (Mary Stewart Van Leeuwen, *Gender and Grace* [Downers Grove, Ill.: InterVarsity Press, 1990], p. 158). Other studies indicate that, later on, a father's availability or absence also affects such things as academic achievement (in sons in particular) and career success (in girls in particular). Of course the benefits to the child's self-esteem are incalculable when there are two adults who are highly involved and available (as opposed to the "exclusive mothering and marginal fathering" that is so common).

pp. 174-75   One couple I know: Told in a personal interview with Rev. Steve Williams and used by permission.

Chapter 9: Finding God in the Midst of Difficulty

pp. 179-80   Abigail would be a perfect candidate: Ruth Tucker, *Multiple Choices* (Grand Rapids: Zondervan, 1992), p. 111.

p. 185   "Pain, if allowed, produces an identification": Tim Hansel, *You Gotta Keep Dancin'* (Elgin, Ill.: David C. Cook, 1985), p. 100.

p. 185   "It's easier to take up a cause": Em Griffin, "What It Takes to Lead People," *Lay Leadership* 3, p. 46.

p. 186   "When we are truly in touch with our ordinariness": From a sermon given by Jim Dethmer at Willow Creek Community Church, October 1990.

p. 187   There is a difference between "good hard" and "destructive hard": My thanks to Bill Hybels for differentiating these categories.

p. 187   Domestic violence is the greatest single cause: Nancy Gibbs, " 'Til Death Do Us Part," *Time,* January 18, 1993, p. 41. This article cited the sobering statistic that in 1991 alone, 4 million women were beaten and 1,320 murdered in domestic attacks.

pp. 187-88   Violence is "a specific choice": James Alsdurf and Phyllis Alsdurf, *Battered into Submission* (Downers Grove, Ill.: InterVarsity Press, 1989), p. 68.

p. 188   "Wives told of being struck": Ibid., pp. 9-10.

p. 188   "The distribution of power": Ibid., p. 17.

pp. 188-89   "After marriage, my husband treated me": Ibid., pp. 17-18

p. 190   "It is too dangerous to discuss": Grant L. Martin, *Counseling for Family Violence and Abuse* (Waco, Tex.: Word, 1987), pp. 99-100.

p. 190   "A woman offers her husband": Alsdurf and Alsdurf, *Battered into Submission,* p. 101.

p. 191   "Life is difficult": M. Scott Peck, *The Road Less Traveled* (New York: Simon & Schuster, 1978), p. 1.

Chapter 10: Reaching Across Generations

p. 195   Paul's use of the word *encourage:* Gene Getz, *The Measure of a Woman* (Ventura, Calif.: Regal, 1977), pp. 59-61.

p. 196   Win Couchman gives an effective image: Win Couchman, "Cross-Generational Relationships," presentation at Women for Christ conference, 1983.

Chapter 11: Being Christ in the World

pp. 212-13   It is hard to comprehend: "In a real sense, not fully comprehensible, the Incarnation gave the already infinitely wise and perfect Son of God the experiential acquisition of knowledge about the human condition. He had to experience the true meaning of obedience in terms of the suffering it entailed. He was thereby made perfect for the role he would play as his people's Captain and High Priest. Suffering thus became a reality that he tasted and from it he can sympathize deeply with his followers" (John E. Walvoord and Roy B. Zuch, eds., *The Bible Knowledge Commentary* [Wheaton, Ill.: Victor, 1983], p. 792).

p. 214   The definition of biblical compassion: W. E. Vine, Merrill F. Unger and William White Jr., eds., *Vine's Expository Dictionary of Biblical Words* (Nashville: Nelson, 1985), pp. 116-17.

p. 217   "No one can help anyone": Henri Nouwen, *The Wounded Healer* (New York: Doubleday, 1979), p. 41.

pp. 218-19   Story of Gladys Acuña, Lisbeth Piedrasanta and the Casa del Alfarero: Ana Gascon Ivey, "Down in the Dumps in Guatemala," *Clarity,* July/August 1994, pp. 31-35.

pp. 219-21   Catherine Booth heard and accepted: Ruth Tucker and Walter Liefeld, *Daughters of the Church* (Grand Rapids: Zondervan, 1987), p. 264; and Norman H. Murdoch, "Female Ministry in the Thought and Work of Catherine Booth," *Church History* 53 (September 1984): 354.

Appendix A: A Look at 1 Timothy 2:11-12 and God's View of Women

p. 224   "According to gnostic thought": Richard Kroeger and Catherine Clark Kroeger, *I Suffer Not a Woman* (Grand Rapids: Baker, 1992), p. 60.

p. 225   Translation of *hesychia:* W. E. Vine, Merrill F. Unger and William White Jr., eds., *Vine's Expository Dictionary of Biblical Words* (Nashville: Nelson, 1985), p. 503.

p. 225   The word *authentein:* The other Greek words translated "authority" in the New Testament are *hyperoche,* meaning "preeminence, superiority, excellency"; *exousia,* meaning "the right to exercise power"; and *epitage,* meaning "command, authority" (ibid).

p. 226   Four meanings of *authentein*: Kroeger and Kroeger, *I Suffer Not a Woman*, p. 84.
p. 226   "To represent oneself as the author:: Ibid., p. 102.
p. 227   "I do not permit": Ibid., p. 103.

About the Author

Ruth Haley Barton is cofounder and president of The Transforming Center <www.thetransformingcenter.org>, a ministry dedicated to caring for the souls of pastors and the congregations they serve. She is a teacher, spiritual director and retreat leader trained through the Shalem Institute for Spiritual Formation (Washington, D.C.) and The Pathways Center for Spiritual Leadership (Nashville).

Educated at Wheaton College and Northern Seminary (Lombard, Illinois), Ruth has served on the pastoral staff of several churches, including Willow Creek Community Church. She has authored numerous articles and books including:

Sacred Rhythms: Arranging Our Lives for Spiritual Transformation (InterVarsity Press)

Invitation to Solitude and Silence: Experiencing God's Transforming Presence (InterVarsity Press)

An Ordinary Day with Jesus: Experiencing the Reality of God in Your Everyday Life (coauthor, Willow Creek Resources)

Equal to the Task: Men and Women in Partnership (InterVarsity Press)

Ruth: Relationships that Bring Life (a Fisherman Bible study, Shaw)

Ruth lives with her husband, Chris, has three daughters and lives in the Chicago area where she spends much of her time teaching, guiding and consulting with leadership groups in the areas of spiritual formation, community building and discernment.

You may contact her at <rhbarton@thetransformingcenter.org>.